JOURNEYS
Evolving Values in the Filipino Diaspora

Stories collected by the

Filipino Association of University Women

(FAUW)

Editors

Virgie Chattergy

Pepi Nieva

DEDICATION

To those who braved journeys to different lands

and to those who will come

after them

ACKNOWLEDGEMENTS

The Filipino Association of University Women of Hawai'i
(FAUW) thanks

Virgie Chattergy, who birthed this collection with her
concept of cultural values and their transmission to the next
generations

Pepi Nieva for editing, layout, and publication.

Rose Cruz Churma for project managing the collection
process

Eduardo Joaquin for designing the book cover

Margot Adair, Edna Alikpala, and Nanette Carreon-Ruhter
for editorial assistance

And all the writers who shared their talents and stories

SALAMAT AND MAHALO.

CONTENTS

Foreword

Journeys

Who We Are

Glossary   About the Cover Artist   FAUW

FOREWORD

Metaphorically speaking, we could say that we all travel in space and through time. In reality, we do travel in real time and occupy space. As we journey, we carry with us our sense of self including material possessions and intangible qualities such as values first learned in earlier years. Core values of our ancestry, although not always easily verbalized, influence our ways of thinking, feeling, and behaving, which in turn shape who we are and what we become.

It's a life-long process, this search for self-knowledge and self-understanding-because it evolves in a continuum from the cradle to the grave. Along the way, depending on circumstances, we keep, modify, or discard values that helped identify us. Such is the challenge for immigrants. It matters little that we ourselves move from our place of ancestral origin to another geographic location, or that we were brought over as a child or born to parents for whom a place is a "host country;" we experience the effects of this transition.

Values that underlie customs and traditions can easily be taken for granted in one's own familiar surroundings but stand out more clearly when experienced in a different setting. Like the process used in our previous book, "Pinay: Culture Bearers of the Filipino Diaspora" published by FAUW (Filipino Association of University Women), invitations went out to Filipinos living abroad to share their stories. This time, contributors were asked specifically to share remembrances of Filipino cultural values in times past and present, with the hope that the younger generation gains some understanding of their ancestral heritage. The contributors who grew up away from their parents' country of origin were encouraged to express their understanding of their elders' "rules" and attitudes or share their concerns or issues encountered as they search for ways to establish their own identity.

Why is FAUW focusing on this theme of Filipino values? The Association's major goal is to cultivate an understanding of Philippine history and culture, and nothing gets to the essence of a people more than what they value. Values provide us with a sense of identity, individually and collectively. They are a source of pride and creates for us a social network. Living out these values ensures the continuity of our cultural and ethnic heritage. Finally, values connect us with our past, give relevance or meaning to our present, and can help direct us as we move forward.

The responses to the call for papers reflect (some expressed clearly, while implied by others) Filipino qualities of resilience, reliance on family and/or community, adaptability, sensitivity, a fighting spirit when called for, a strong sense of faith that things will work out somehow, and a lightness of spirit. If one or more of these very diverse stories help our younger Filipinos gain deeper insight into his/her ancestry, FAUW will have attained its goal.

Virgie Chattergy
Co-editor

Readers of our first volume, "Pinay: Culture Bearers of the Filipino Diaspora," mentioned the need for definitions for those who might not be familiar with Filipino values. In Philippine schools, we learned basic values such as:

Bahala na or leave it to God (inshallah).

Pakikisama: getting along and cooperating with others which cultivates another value—smooth interpersonal relationships.

Utang na loob: reciprocity and paying back with gratitude.

Amor propio: self love or esteem. Wounded amor propio can lead to the value of pakikibaka or fighting resistance.

Hiya, translated into shame by earlier scholars, is given a more recent, outward-oriented definition: feeling that one is in a socially unacceptable position.

Bayanihan: spirit of community and helping others.

Influential social scientist Virgilio Enriquez designated an overarching value that encompasses many of the above: the concept of kapwa—sharing of self with others, or shared sense of identity in a collective society.

Year-long research by the Philippine National Commission on Culture and the Arts identified 19 core values, in "A Study on Filipino Values (A Primer)," published in 2020. Topping the list were family, education, and faith. These align with a 1996 World Values Survey which identified family, religion, and work as the three most cherished Filipino values.

The stories in this book certainly reflect the results of these studies. It remains to be seen how these values will evolve as Filipinos adapt to their new environments. Even the meanings of values change depending on who is perceiving and who is practicing them. For example, while bahala na was described as fatalism by western sociologists; according to more contemporary Filipino scholars, this value allows risk taking and resourceful problem solving in uncertain situations where predicting the future is near to impossible.

This book's representation of the experiences of the Filipino in diaspora is somewhat limited because most of our authors are older, in fields such as education and nursing, who perhaps have a greater propensity to writing. Most are FAUW members and their colleagues and friends. We have two essays from descendants of sakada, the Filipino migrant workers of Hawai'i; they transcended their humble beginnings through education, ambition, and hard work. We need more stories from

4

amazon Gift Receipt

Send a Thank You Note

You can learn more about your gift or start a return here too.

Scan using the Amazon app or visit
https://a.co/d/5sJyLPa

JOURNEYS: Evolving Values in the Filipino Diaspora
Order ID: 112-2648800-3488269   Ordered on March 7, 2023

younger Filipinos, OFWs (overseas workers), and those belonging to more diverse demographics.

Our book is divided into two sections.

In *Journeys*, we travel with the authors as they reminisce about their hometowns, the different ways they left the Philippines, and what they found in their new homes "abroad."

Part two, *Who We Are*, demonstrates different circumstances and approaches to finding identity in the diaspora.

As in our first volume, "Pinay," we did not italicize Pilipino and most non-English words. Hopefully, the glossary in the back of this book will suffice to increase the readers' understanding, as well as vocabulary!

Comments and reactions are welcome! Email them to fauw1987@gmail.com.

Pepi Nieva
Co-editor

JOURNEYS

Bayong, carryall basket.

One

TRADITIONAL VALUES IN A NON-TRADITIONAL WORLD

by Rolando Santos, Ph.D

Some traditional Filipino values persist through generations. However, they may differ in their manifestations in a changing world and in changing family circumstances. Some values learned from our parents and grandparents are being revised or replaced by contrary values learned from peers, communication media, economic situations, and new educational insights in a modern world where traditional values call for adaptations or face outright rejection.

Now, I am miles and decades away from Zamboanga City in Southern Philippines where I was born. During World War II, I started my first four years of elementary schooling in the towns of Isabela and Lamitan on Basilan Island. After the war, I finished upper elementary, secondary, and undergraduate education in Zamboanga City. When I was 23 years old, I was awarded a Smith-Mundt/Fulbright Scholarship to study in the U.S. where, after four years, I earned an M.A. and Ph.D. degrees. During those years, I also managed to work and travel for extended periods of time in several countries around the world. In 1962, I returned to the Philippines and, in the next three years, taught in Mindanao State College, Bicol Teachers College, Baguio Vacation Normal School, and the University of the Philippines. In the meantime, I married Karen Long who was a Peace Corps volunteer in the Bicol region during my year teaching there.

The traditional Santoses of Zamboanga; Rolando and Karen's wedding; the non-traditional Santoses of California.

7

Karen was from Nebraska. She and I clicked very well despite the differences in backgrounds. She is of German-Dutch lineage, and I a Filipino-Spanish Basque mestizo. She grew up in a farming town of Diller with a population of less than 300 and I from a port city with a population of almost a million. She is Lutheran, and I am Catholic. Diller is a homogeneous, monolingual town and Zamboanga is multiethnic and multilingual.

This was the multicultural context within which Karen and I raised three sons and a daughter. Two sons were born in Manila but left with us for the U.S.; Rolsky was two years old and Ricky a few months old. In the U.S., we resided in neighborhoods where there were no Filipino neighbors and had infrequent contacts with Filipino expats, most of whose children were also born and raised in the U.S. In later years, we, with the kids visited the Philippines and met several relatives and friends in Zamboanga, Basilan, and Manila. Those experiences helped the children define themselves as they observed others respond to their looks, their English, their manners, and mannerisms. In their short visits with Karen's family, the kids also experienced the Nebraska side's cultural origins and orientations. After seven years, we moved into our permanent residence in San Marino, an upscale, and predominantly white neighborhood—a world of new peers and experiences with new lifestyles.

With strands of cultural values from the Philippines and Nebraska, and influences from California peers, teachers, and athletic coaches, what are our children and grandchildren weaving into the fabric of their lives?

Family Ties

Family unity has been a central value in my youth and persists today with my children and grandchildren. During the war, without radio, TV, newspapers, and neighbors around, the family was the sole nurturer, provider, and defender for my brother Jun and me. He and I had only each other to play with.

9

My parents, a grandmother, and a maid made up our family unit. Eventually, three more children were born. Times changed at war's end. Our household grew when homeless and unemployed relatives sought relief by staying with us in our rented houses. Our paternal home had burned down early during the war. For me, that extended-family arrangement lasted until I was 23 years old when I left home to study in the U.S.

However, that physical independence from the family did not end the extended-family connections. My new life does not necessarily involve physical closeness, but modern communication technology and the global economy may be fostering stronger family ties without the day-to-day irritants endemic in multigenerational households. After college, our kids lived and worked away from our home and later established their own businesses and their own nuclear-family residences. Their spouses are all Americans.

Our three sons married blondes and my daughter a brunette. All live in their own private residences in the U.S., although Rick and his family have their main residence in the Philippines. We hear from all of them from any place in the world they are in and keep abreast of their activities on Facebook, e-Mail, Instagram, FaceTime, and other communication media. Our ten grandchildren are in different educational institutions in the U.S. Their occasional visits to our home in San Marino, either on the way from or to their respective homes on business and leisure trips, have helped maintain our strong family ties.

Family Dynamics

Traditionally, family authority flowed downward from the parents and older siblings. Grandparents gave advice but did not have final say on family matters. As my mother used to say to her mother, "Ma, you have raised your children. Now let me raise mine!" In the family, the women are not subservient to men. As my father said, "I only decide where the atom bomb will be dropped. My wife makes all other decisions!" The use of honorifics with parents, grandparents, and other elders has been obligatory.

Smooth interpersonal relations are very important considerations in individual interactions. Although they may have had their differences, I never heard my parents confront each other or my grandparents. Nor have I ever had any confrontations with my children and grandchildren. That also has meant no corporal punishment administered. When pushed to the limit, however, when one's amor propio (ego) is hurt, occasional lashing out occurs. Giving the silent treatment is preferred. In multi-generational households where physical closeness is inevitable, this value is most critical. Everyone has to be a diplomat! This silence may last for long periods when neither party is willing to lose face by giving in. Sometimes, it takes a third party to intercede and end the silence.

Church and Religion

All through my childhood and early youth, our lives followed closely church liturgy, marking the seasons and days commemorating the lives and virtues of Christ and Saints. Family daily prayers, masses on holy days of obligation, confessions, communions, religious processions, prayers for the dead, town fiestas, and other religious observances were religiously observed.

The role of religion in the lives of the children and grandchildren has changed much from the observances of my early years. I have not been much of a model for my children and grandchildren in the practice of any religious faith despite my early family experiences and Jesuit educational training and Karen's Lutheran upbringing. However, I admire the integrity, bereft of all the conflicting issues of doctrine, sophistry, practice, precepts, and prescriptions, that marks the lives of our children and grandchildren.

Hospitality

Invited or not, expected or unexpected, visitors can expect to be offered something to eat or drink, even if it means borrowing something to offer the visitor from next-door neighbors. Normally, when a visitor shows up unexpectedly during mealtime, the guest would be invited to join in or the family would postpone eating until the company leaves.

On a town fiesta day, lavish meals are usually served to all those dropping by. Often, the cost of such generosity could be so expensive that loans would be taken out to finance the feast and avoid being criticized as being kuriput (stingy). That would be nakakahiya (shameful). Some families just close up their homes and leave town to avoid the onerous cost involved in feeding everybody who shows up, expected or not.

My children and grandchildren freely invite friends for home cookouts and might have friends for sleepovers, or they spend weekends in their friends' vacation homes, yachts, or mountain lodges, or spend vacation time with friends on special occasions. However, gone are the days when, in my ancestral home, relatives or family acquaintances would just show up with their bags and ask to stay, expecting to be supported by my parents and grandparents. Some would stay for days, some for months or years! Those were desperate times of the depression and World War II and people sought out any refuge to ensure their well-being. There was no government welfare system and employment possibilities were limited. When good jobs were available, usually relatives or children of compadres (relatives by affinity) were hired over unrelated, even if more qualified, applicants.

Child Rearing

Growing up in the Philippines was growing up in the world of adults. Children were to be seen and not heard! I don't remember learning from my grandfathers. I don't remember even being hugged or coddled by them as a child. My grandmothers just made sure we ate well and learned our prayers and were well-behaved. They emphasized the importance of being obedient and respectful. From the yayas (maids or

12

nannies), we were warned of evil blood-sucking spirits lurking in the dark, in huge trees, in earthen mounds, and in other sinister places, haunting disobedient and disrespectful children! Beware of the aswang, the buruju, the nunu, the kapre, and the duende! We also had the comic-strip worlds of Tarzan, Batman and Robin, Superman, King Kong, and Dracula! Our kids and grandkids did not grow up with those evil spirits and comic strips. However, they grew up with their own fantasies—tooth fairies, Easter bunnies, Santa Claus and his reindeer. Of course, there were the extra-terrestrial creatures, the Unidentified Flying Objects, and pre-historical monsters terrorizing earthlings! With the computers came "Star Wars" and new gaming adventures. Now, those who have outgrown their childhood fantasies are concerned with SPORTS! The craving for entertainment remains but replaced by other venues.

Education

My father earned his teaching credential at the Zamboanga Normal School and my mother from the Philippine Normal School in Manila. Father eventually became an elementary school principal, and for several years served as secret service chief and eventually chief of police. Mother was an academic supervisor. All of us children, except one, had college degrees. The one who did not, served as steward in the U.S. Navy. That was a great family disappointment.

When we had our own children, I promised that whatever and wherever they decided to study, I would support them. I did not want to be blamed for any failure in getting what and where they got their education. So, they took me up on that promise! With great effort and sacrifice on our part, some financial assistance from Karen's parents and aunt, and part-time work on the children's part, they got all the degrees they wanted from institutions of their choice.

They have not let us down: Rolsky graduated from San Diego State University; Ricky from U.C. Berkeley, London

School of Economics, and Oxford University; Lani from UCLA and special studies at Cambridge University; and Robbie, our youngest son, from Harvard. Our eldest grandchild, Ryan, is also at Harvard. Reed is at Babson College, Jordan at Northeastern University, Hunter at University of Oregon, and Rand at U.C. Berkeley. Five others are still in elementary and high schools.

Academic performance is given much importance. Grade point average and SAT test scores are important for college admission. In subjects where the grandchildren are weak, private tutors are hired. During my school days, when I needed help, I would seek it from classmates. Usually, whatever help I needed in those subjects were far above what my parents could help me with and paid tutors were unheard of.

Sports

The development of physical skills of my brother and me seemed of little concern in the family. Our family was just focused on our physical safety. On my own, I learned how to swim, bike, roller skate, climb trees, and sail a canoe. I wanted so badly to attend the local public schools where I could participate in track-and-field competition. City, regional, and national athletic meets were only for public schools. The folks insisted that we attend the Ateneo, the local private Jesuit school— prestigious, academic, and religious. All we had at the Ateneo were intramural sports. My father had a group of his friends that played softball. No children were included. There were no organized games for children anywhere in town and, whatever sports the adults participated in never included children—too dangerous and we might get hurt! Of course, there was no television then and radio news reports made no mention of any athletic activities.

Our children played with the neighborhood kids but were too young for any organized team sports when we first arrived in the U.S. Then we moved to San Marino, an exclusive residential city in San Gabriel valley made prestigious by the Henry

Huntington Gardens and Library and former residence of George Patton adjacent to the Huntington estate. Rolsky and Ricky wanted to sign up to play in the local baseball Little League. We did not approve because they might get hurt! Instead, we took them to parks, public libraries, Disneyland, Knotts Berry Farm, and beaches where they would be safe! We noticed, however, that, at the end of their school days, they would sit on our doorsteps watching their friends in their baseball uniforms riding their bikes to play baseball in the school grounds. Ricky complained saying. "Dad, you were born in the wrong place and the wrong time!"

Gradually, Karen and I became concerned about how much damage we were inflicting on the kids' psychological well-being by not allowing them to play. Eventually, we relented and, incredibly, they excelled in Little League baseball, soccer, and track. In university-level sports and in international competitions, they starred in soccer, football, rugby, and track. Ironically, Karen and I have gotten so involved in the sports activities of the children and grandchildren that often we have changed our work, social, and travel schedules to watch their games.

Money Management

Getting regular money allowances was unheard of when we were children. Children were not paid for doing home chores. It was considered family responsibility. If any chores had to be done, there were servants to do them! In brief, we kids never got paid for anything! To have asked to be paid would have been sin vergüenza (shameless). If we needed something that mother approved of and money was available, she would just give us the money. It was war time and there was nothing to buy except some snacks from street vendors. And there was no regular income for us to count on and so there was nothing to budget for! Even after the war, when we could have additional income, my siblings and I did not look for jobs.

In the U.S. when our four kids were of high school and

college age, they chose to work part-time for extra pocket money in food outlets, surf shops, department stores, and campus jobs. Traditionally, in the social-class conscious culture of Filipino society, those "menial" jobs were considered inappropriate for persons considered of a higher class. Until I went to the U.S., I was a señorito. However, despite the fact that I had generous financial grants and didn't need any financial help, I worked as a waiter in the university cafeteria. On campus, it was a plum job and I wanted an experience that I would not have in the Philippines! There was no pay but the meals were free. That meant a lot of savings for me. There was no embarrassment in doing cafeteria work; that kind of work is not considered demeaning in the U.S. Our grandchildren who were born and grew up in the U.S. also have been working part time. Their first cousins, born and raised in the Philippines, did not do any of that type of jobs. Instead, they did internships in corporations during summer breaks—no "menial" jobs for them.

Traditional Values: Uses and Abuses

Values are neutral in the abstract. They can be practiced for good or for bad. Often, when laws conflict with the beliefs and values of a people, traditional mores prevail. Family unity, for instance, is a value that could be good when it provides for family members' welfare. But it also could encourage parasitism and foster favoritism over meritocratic criterion for employment or in politics. Respect for authority could ease social relationships but could also lead to abuses by government officials, clergy, and others in authority. Bahala na (whatever may be) attitude may foster peace of mind but may also sap initiative. Utang na loob (reciprocity) fosters gratitude for benefits received but also can encourage graft, corruption, and abuse of power. Smooth interpersonal relations considerations may be comfortable but encourage deceit and misunderstanding. In dealing with social evils, silence could mean approval. Emphasis on a person's family lineage, skin color, and religious beliefs may help ensure family unity but this elitism may poison social relationships and impede upward social mobility.

Despite my light Spanish-mestizo color, in the American South where I was studying, I was considered colored and subjected to Jim Crow segregation laws. Racism also plagued me in other parts of the country. When I married Karen, her state of Nebraska was one of several that had anti-miscegenation laws. It was against the law for a Nebraskan to marry a Filipino or any other colored person. My children and grandchildren have not had to face that degradation. They all look and speak American!

Filipinized

In most of my public presentations, the audiences love to hear about Filipino culture and my experiences as a Filipino in America. I learned Filipino dances and songs and wear barong Tagalog, none of which I had done in the Philippines. I studied more intently Philippine history to put in perspective our varied past. During my teenage years I liked everything American—Hollywood movies, American songs and dances, English language not Tagalog (Pilipino). In retrospect, I realize how I had been Americanized in the Philippines and Filipinized in the US.

Now our children and grandchildren go to the internet to get recipes for traditional native dishes, check out Philippine resorts on many of the islands, as well as search for their cultural and historical backgrounds for their school reports. There definitely are traces of Filipino values in my children and grandchildren even if, at times, those strains may be subtle and undetectable to family outsiders. We all enjoy pancit, adobo, and lumpia and proudly wear barong Tagalog and terno whenever appropriate. Whenever my son's company in Manila celebrates big events, many international guests also wear Filipino attire and enjoy the performance of the Tinikling, the Philippine bamboo dance.

Rick and sons have dual citizenship—Filipino and American. Other family members and I are just Americans! When I became an American citizen, according to the law then I had to renounce Philippine citizenship. That was a difficult decision. The swearing-in ceremony was a sad occasion for me and there was no celebration. I don't even have a single photo of the event. However, I remind myself that, if we had stayed in the Philippines, we would not have accomplished as much as we have. Opportunities would have been limited.

A closer look at the dynamics of values transmission and the study of family trees are interesting academic exercises but do not fully explain why some fruits do not fall far from the tree and others do when, like in my family, there are several trees involved—my ancestry, my wife's, our sons and daughter, and grandchildren. What is most important is that everyone grows up and raises their own progeny as thoughtful and productive human beings regardless of family origins.

*An engaging raconteur, **Rolando Santos** analyzes with heart and humor the dynamics of the transmission of traditional Filipino values in the context of his biracial family and worldwide travels and work. He taught at the California State University, Los Angeles until his retirement as professor emeritus after 43 years. He served as visiting professor and lecturer in other colleges and universities in the U.S. and abroad, authored a book on "Chavacano de Zamboanga," and lists as his hobbies traveling, reading, writing, music, ballroom dancing, gardening, watching athletic competitions, TV news reports and historical reviews, and collects Filipino, Spanish, Latin American, Italian, and American folk art and antiquities.*

Two

A LIFE BETWEEN

by Belinda A Aquino, Ph.D

If this narrative sounds like a memoir, it is not meant to be. I used the above title, which needs a bit of explaining especially the phrase "life between," because that can mean a lot of numerous spaces and stages of events in my life.

The space I am writing in is more than, and not necessarily, geographical as in the Philippines and America. This "life between" is a situational and dynamic one, subject to constant changes and extreme contrasts during entire lifetimes and generations.

As psychologist Erik Ericson notes in his various writings on the American identity, "most inhabitants are faced, in their own lives or within the orbit of their close relatives, with alternatives presented by such polarities as open roads of immigration and jealous islands of traditions; outgoing internationalism and defiant isolationism; boisterous competition and self-effacing cooperation..." ("Childhood and Society," 2nd ed. New York: Norton and Co.,1963: 285). In a major and substantial way, this is how I would characterize my "life between."

I am essentially a product of public schools in my hometown, a situation that I consider the basis of my secular and socialized identity. In comparison, many of my peers and cohorts entered private schools with a religious or sectarian orientation.

19

In Philippine society and culture, especially when I was growing up in the 1950s, the concept of choice was essentially non-existent. Decisions were made for you by your parents, relatives, teachers, and others whose role was to tell you what to do. That was why from elementary and high school. life was fairly uniform and agreeable. We even wore uniforms to underscore this basic culture of obedience and propriety. There was no escaping it because you did not exist by yourself. You belonged to a large family, a clan, and a village, and you were never alone for most of your young life.

Breaking Away

It was an unusual and individual act of rebellion on my part to break away from this debilitating pattern of young adulthood. As far as identity is concerned, I consider rebellion as a personal trait; a combined curiosity about the world outside, a rejection of some but not all traditional norms and values; and a sense of "come what may."

I made certain, however, that this attitude should not be equated to the common bahala na (the English equivalent of the come what may) escape route. Not that I was running away from an oppressive existence or something that some western analysts might attribute to a domineering mother, authoritarian father, or some pathological or dysfunctional aspect of family socialization. I just thought that there was another set of basic truths and values out there beyond the confines of a small town or village.

So leaving my hometown for Manila, the Big City 200 miles away, was the first significant change in my young life. And for the first time, I became conscious of an emerging "life between" my regional identity as an Ilocano and another world within university walls.

I was exposed to a multiplicity of ethnicities at the University of the Philippines campus. I ended up in a boarding house or cottage with five other students from Surigao del Sur in the Mindanao region. They occupied the main room in the cottage, and I and another Ilocana, who was a distant relative, were in the smaller room.

Lindy as a student in Manila.

The loud chatter of the five girls speaking in Cebuano, a Visayan language, amused me. At times, I was picking up some of their conversations and eventually understood what they were talking about. But we ended up communicating more effectively in English and we also conversed in Tagalog or Pilipino, the Philippine national language taught in my high school. Eventually, I met students from all over the Philippine regions—Tagalog, Kapampangan, Ilonggo, Bicolano, Waray, and so on. It was at times more effective to combine Tagalog with words from the different areas of the Philippines. It was also more fun mixing up all our various languages (there are about eight different Philippine languages and dozens of dialects).

I became a member of the University of the Philippines Student Catholic Action club and attended Catholic mass regularly, always remembering my mother's advice to pray especially because I was now far away from home. Occasionally, she would visit me from the province, bringing a lot of food and supplies. I was experiencing a "brave new world" so different and a bit intimidating from my old hometown.

I also felt a growing consciousness from participating in campus politics. Student activism was developing with and among various campus constituencies and the fraternities and sororities on campus. I made sure I gave priority to my studies because there were a lot of requirements needed for graduation, including foreign languages such as French, German, or Latin and, for English majors like me, natural and social sciences. We also had to take a lot of classes on American History, which were interesting because they were not like those we took in high school. These courses were mostly American colonial history, extolling American heroes like George Washington and Abraham Lincoln. I struggled to complete a college degree that would land me a good job later and prepare me for another chapter: life in the real world.

Coming to America

When I finished college in the late 1950s, the first thought that came to my mind was a job. However, I was not sure what kind of work I could get with a Bachelor of Arts in the Humanities with a major in English.

I did not even have enough Education courses to qualify me to teach at the high school level. I was at another "life between" crossroad and I finally decided to go back to college to specialize in some field that could qualify me for a decent paying job.

I chose the field of Public Administration at the University of the Philippines Institute Administration, which offered a number of graduate fellowships. I received a grant that allowed me to take courses on Government, Personnel and Fiscal Administration, National-Local Relations, and related fields. I began to learn more about another area of human knowledge: social science, quite different from my undergraduate major in the Humanities and its focus on Shakespeare, Melville, Emerson, Thoreau, and the whole New England gang of notable writers and authors. It was completely disorienting for me at first but I had gotten used to a "life between" at this stage.

I started to understand more about the intricate and bureaucratic processes and nuances involved in the various levels of government from the presidency down to the lowest unit of governance, the village, or the barrio as it is called in the Philippines.

Lindy as Philippine Studies director.

Then another opening for a scholarship opened up, this time from the Fulbright and East-West Center in the early 1960s. I applied for a master's degree in Political Science at the University of Hawai'i at Manoa. The Department of Political Science was especially interested in attracting applicants from the Asia-Pacific region. I went on to complete a doctoral degree from Cornell University after which I looked forward to returning to the Philippines to resume my faculty duties at the University of the Philippines. I thought that living permanently in my own country would be the end of my continuously "swinging" life. This would have been a logical conclusion to what had been a hectic back-and-forth experience and it would be a relief to settle in my native land that I had only visited occasionally while studying in Hawai'i.

Martial Law Intervenes

But it was not to be. A major event made me change my plans midstream. In September 1973, then President Ferdinand Marcos declared Martial Law, using the continuing aggression of the leftwing underground forces and the Muslim insurgency in Mindanao as his reasons for emergency rule.

Marcos had instructed the Philippine Embassy in Washington D.C. to infiltrate a conference in Cornell attended by some 150 Filipino students, myself included, studying in various U.S. institutions. These students organized a conference about discussing alternatives to Martial Law. The order from Malacanang was to cancel their Philippine passports. To my surprise, I landed on the "blacklist" of Filipino students "whose activities in the U.S. were considered inimical to the national security of the Philippines." The Philippine Consulate had been spying on students who were active in organizations resisting the regime like the Movement for a Free Philippines, Union of Democratic Filipinos, the Friends of the Filipino People, and Ninoy Aquino Movement (NAM).

Lindy at rally with Jose Limon.

Without a passport, I could not go back to the Philippines. My only recourse was to stay in the U.S., another "life between." The problem was I was summarily served with a letter from the Immigration and Naturalization Service (INS) to explain why I should not be deported since my student visa had expired after I finished my degree in Cornell. The INS called me to a trial-like hearing.

This was a real "in-between" dilemma—deportable from the U.S. and undesirable on the Philippine end. I hired a pro-bono defense lawyer who studied my case. She found a provision in the immigration law which might be acceptable to "stay my execution."

I could apply for "suspension of deportation" if I had lived seven years in America. What this meant was the longer I stayed in the U.S. with this case hanging over my head, the better since it would buy me some time to fulfill the seven-year proviso.

At this point, my lawyer and I decided to contact Congresswoman Patsy T. Mink to seek her advice. I had worked on her various political campaigns in Hawai'i. She suggested that we also seek U.S. Senator Daniel K. Inouye's help as only senators can introduce a private bill for individuals who deserve to remain in the United States. I was getting an education on the nuances of American bureaucratic processes of seeking redress for cases similar to mine.

To cut a long story short, on March 18, 1976 at the 74th Congress, Senator Inouye introduced Senate Bill 3175, my private bill. It stated that "for purposes of the Immigration and Nationality Act, Dr. Belinda A. Aquino shall be held and considered to have been admitted to the United States for permanent residence as of the date of enactment of this Act, upon payment of the required visa fee."

A few years after having acquired permanent residence status, I filed for U.S. citizenship. At least, that would stop my back-and-forth "life between" the Philippines and the United States. I had to prove that I was of good moral character, had a steady job with the faculty of the University of Hawai'i, paid my taxes, and that there was no possibility that I would be a public charge. I had to get all kinds of letters from prominent individuals who would attest to the viability and merit of my application.

A few weeks after fulfilling all the citizenship requirements, my approval letter arrived via special delivery from the White House. It read:

Dear Fellow American:

I am pleased to congratulate you on becoming a United States citizen. You are now a part of a great and blessed nation. I know your family and friends are proud of you on this special day.

Welcome to the joy, responsibility, and freedom of American citizenship, God bless you, and God bless America.

Sincerely,

GEORGE W. BUSH

Happy Ending

This in a nutshell is the saga of my journey through a "life between." I take one hard look at my life events in terms of the Filipino global diaspora. What Filipino values have played in living at the crossroads?

My desire for higher education led to breaking away from familiar home ground to a more complex society. In the process, a different consciousness took root with its own set of complex values. You encounter and accept new norms without necessarily rejecting old ones. This is all part of the dynamic process called socialization. As you develop an adult identity, you discover new ways of thinking to further alter your earlier beliefs and behavior.

Life is full of surprises along the way. The declaration of Martial Law in the Philippines in the early 1970s and my being in the blacklist of the Marcos regime, along with my expired student visa, put me between a rock and a hard place. With the help of a State representative, a senator, and legal loopholes, I was able to remain on American soil. Sometimes, I laugh at my "life between" and the twists and turns that enabled me to come to America. But "all's well that ends well."

Dr. Belinda (Lindy) Aquino *is a professor emeritus at the University of Hawai'i at Mānoa where she served as professor of Political Science and Asian Studies for nearly 40 years before retiring. Lindy received her PhD in Political Science from Cornell University as a Ford Foundation Fellow. She was the founding director of the University of Hawai'i Center for Philippine Studies. She was also a visiting professor, scholar, and research fellow at the Tokyo University of Foreign Studies; Institute of Southeast Asian Studies in Singapore; Thammasat University in Bangkok, Thailand; and in four universities in Indonesia.*

Three

ALPHABET SOUP

By *Conchita Schlemmer, LCSW*

Let me back up a little. My name is Conchita Palomera Villafuerte Schlemmer. I was born in Manila, Philippines. My parents are Antonio and Concepcion P. Villafuerte. I am the fifth child in a family of six: three older brothers, one older sister, and another brother ten years younger than me. During the ten years when I was the youngest, my older siblings tended to keep me hopping. "Chit, do this, get me this." But they were protective of me. I spent my early childhood in Tayabas and Lucena, Quezon province, later moving to Manila after the war. I decided to write down the recollections and reflections of an old lady who is a Mom, Ate, Tita, and Lola Chit to the family.

I attended the Instituto de Mujeres, Legarda Elementary School, Santo Tomas High School, and the Far Eastern University. I went to the Ateneo Graduate School in Padre Faura, Manila for my graduate studies in Psychology. It was there where a mentor, Fr. Jaime Bulatao, SJ, inspired and encouraged me to go abroad. At this time too, my relationship with my boyfriend, who had left for New York for his medical residency, ended.

I was the first in my family to leave the nest for an adventure in a far-away land. My father was not in favor of the move, but my mother was very supportive and encouraging. Before leaving Manila, it was customary then to get a brief orientation to the ways and mores of the new place. We learned the cultural oddities of western ways of eating, greetings, communicating, being open and assertive, (which took me a long time to develop). Like everyone, I carried that big chest X-ray board on the plane, a mandate for everyone entering the U.S. to prevent the spread of tuberculosis.

In 1964, I was accepted as an intern in Clinical Psychology at the Hawai'i State Hospital (HSH) in Kaneohe. When I first saw the Koolau mountain range, I was moved by its awesome beauty, with its waterfalls cascading down the ridges of the velvety green mountains. I instantly fell in love with the island. It was love at first sight.

At that time, the HSH was full of resident psychiatric patients as there were no out-patient clinics yet. There were two interns from the Philippines, Gloria and I, and we were only the ones with master's degrees. We were provided board and lodging, but no stipends, as these were for U.S. citizens only. We were accepted because of our language capacity that enabled us to work with older Filipino patients who had difficulties with English. Three other PhD interns were from U.S. mainland universities.

We stayed at the dorm on the hospital compound, which is now the Windward Community College. I loved the food at the dining hall. I thought it was delicious, balanced, and new to my taste. Other interns and staff thought it tasted like "institutional food."

Every day as I walked up towards the dining hall and the wards, I remember admiring the mountain behind the hospital. Its beauty and lush greenery were so close, within your grasp, and I wondered, "How can people stay crazy in this place!"

My first experience with cultural differences was the way my supervisors, all PhDs in Psychology, preferred to be called by their first names instead of being addressed as "doctor." They were very supportive, comfortable, casual (feet on their desks— shocking!), and very willing and eager to teach. This was my first

Wedding day: the bride took a cab to church.

exposure to who, in the Philippines, we called "foreigners" (Caucasians). I found them accepting and friendly. In one of our monthly group sessions, consisting of resident psychiatrists and interns, one doctor stated that I reminded her of a lotus flower blossom as I was quiet, yet dignified. I felt good and that seems to have defined my demeanor ever since.

That December in 1964, one of my co-interns, Len Elkins, a Jewish guy from New York invited me to a Christmas party up in Tantalus Heights. There I met Christine, a young woman of Japanese descent, who spoke with strong Japanese accent. She and I became good friends and hung out on weekends. She drove a convertible Triumph sports car, and riding in the topdown was an exhilarating experience for a naive, shy, and simple girl from the Philippines. We had a blast! Christine worked as a secretary to the CEO of the McWayne Marine Supply. It was Christine who eventually introduced me to my husband Allan, who was working as a marine engine mechanic for the company.

It was April 16, 1966 when we got married at the Sacred Heart Church on Wilder Avenue. Early that morning, I went to a beauty parlor and did not tell the hairdresser about the significance of that day. All by myself without any family around to help, I put on my makeup and the wedding gown designed, sewn, and mailed from the Philippines by my sister-in-law. My friend and maid of honor Vicky de la Cruz and I took a cab to the church.

The Schlemmers: Rachel and Allan Jr, Eric and Cinda, Chit, Allan, Sr.

When I first informed my family of my plan to get married, my oldest brother Tony wrote back telling me to come home; he said I was just home sick. As I had no family in Hawai'i then, my supervisor, Dr.Gudeman walked me to the altar. The guests were Al's family and my handful of friends, but I felt the wedding was perfect, simple, and elegant. A reception was held at Al's parents beautiful house on Lewalani Drive in Makiki. There was music, a regular routine when the Schlemmers get together: Auntie Helene on the piano, and the brothers and

31

sisters singing along. No dancing or pinning of money, the Filipino way.

The Schlemmers are an old kamaaina family. Al's grandfather, Max, was the chief of police who guarded Queen Lili'uokalani. He is also the manager of guano production on Laysan Island, now a national reserve. Although my marriage is bi-racial and bi-cultural, there are more similarities than differences. Al's mother (Portuguese) is Catholic, and his dad (German) is non -practicing Christian. They agreed to raise all their children as Catholics. His dad's famous saying is, "The world is my church and to do good is my religion." He is a good and lovable man. Both Al and I value love of family, a good education for the kids, and our Catholic traditions.

I had a near-death experience when I gave birth to our first son, Eric, at the old Kaiser hospital in Waikiki, now the site of the Prince Hotel. I saw the triangular shape of bright, bright, lights (the Holy Trinity symbols), and I remember asking God to send me back. I wanted to raise my son. I promised to be a nun!

Eric now has a daughter and is grandfather of two. He works in a refinery, resides in Washington state, and owns several homes and rental units. Our second son Allan Jr., Junjor for short, was born in Manila where we went to build a contact lens business. It didn't pan out, but I remember my family was so happy to see us. I went to so many parties, ate so much palabok and halo-halo, and gained so much weight that when we delivered Junjor at the St. Luke's Hospital, he was so big (about 10 pounds, 21 inches) the doctor had to use forceps. He came out all bruised up! Now he is 6'2 tall, healthy, creative, and happily living with his wife Rachel in New York City.

Our youngest daughter Lisa was diagnosed with Congenital Rubella Syndrome. I was apparently exposed to the German measles, during my first trimester. She is deaf, blind, and mentally challenged. She now resides with a loving foster family who takes good care of her. She comes home every other weekend and we continue to be involved as her parents and legal guardians.

I now affirm how my faith and spirituality, strong determination, and bahala na outlook enabled and sustained me during difficult times. When Filipinos say bahala na, we say we are leaving our concerns and problems to God (Bathala in the Pilipino language). Relying on faith and accepting fate strengthens coping skills. This is contrary to the western emphasis on self-determination and self-actualization.

My career has an expanse of 40 years since I graduated from University of Hawai'i, Manoa with a master's in Social Work in 1975. My first job was as a project director of the Immigrant Services Program at Susannah Wesley Community Center, a non-profit social service agency that aims to help newcomers from various countries become contributing members of the community. I designed and implemented a multi-faceted program for recent immigrants in the Kalihi-Palama area, a neighborhood in Honolulu where many newly arrived residents begin their life in the State.

I had a staff of three Filipino, two Korean, and two Samoan outreach workers. We assisted our clients in applying for jobs, medical services, food stamps, bus passes, and more. Advocating for their children in school was very helpful. Personal counseling on parenting and conflicting cultural values was also beneficial.

It's true one can leave a country, but the country does not leave the individual. We feel, think, and behave ethnically. We want to communicate with our own languages, form friendships with people like us, and eat the food of our hometowns. Ethnocentricity appears common to all cultures. Drastic change to one's way of life is not easy, but people do adapt to their environment.

One of the seminars, I was invited to focus on the various cultural backgrounds of our clients and how the providers can better serve them. I shared my thoughts on Filipino cultural beliefs and practices. The early Filipino migrants to Hawaiʻi arrived as plantation workers. With the liberalization of U.S. immigration laws in 1965, more Filipinos came to the islands, many as relatives of the earlier immigrants. Professionals such as doctors and skilled workers also came under the new laws.

Dr. Danilo Ponce, in his book "People and Cultures of Hawaiʻi," expounded on four distinct cultural characteristics that may be valuable in understanding Filipino behavior: amor propio (self-esteem), hiya (shame), pakikisama (smooth inter-personal relations), and utang na loob (indebtedness/gratitude). Not all Filipinos may exhibit these values in the same way due to factors like geographical origins: rural vs. urban, for example. Recognizing regional differences is important, as are socio-economic status, educational background, and circumstances of coming to Hawaiʻi.

I found that to work effectively with Filipinos, providers must exude warmth. They may have to assert authority in the initial stage of the working relationship. While there is a need for a lot of clarification and interpretation, Filipinos respond more to direct, concrete, problem-solving strategies. Opening up by clients is a long and slow process, but once a personal relationship is established, one can work effectively with them.

As a clinician, I realized how cloistered I was when, to my surprise, we had cases of Filipino fathers abusing their daughters. I learned to work with the abused children—rebuilding self-esteem, self-worth, and body image; empowering them and their mothers, mostly abused themselves, to protect themselves, be more assertive and supportive of their children. Most of the perpetrators, with the help of the court's mandated counseling, finally were able to admit their wrongs, stop the abuse, and eventually write a letter of apology to their child and family.

During the early part of my career, I remember feeling intimidated and patronized when I was assigned only to Filipino clients. I wanted the challenge of working with other ethnic groups with various diagnoses, problems, and concerns, using my knowledge and training on various approaches in therapy. Later, at the State Department of Human Services, Judiciary, and the State Department of Health's Mental Health Division I was able to do that. I worked with abused children and adults, domestic violence victims, foster placements, and dysfunctional couples and families. I pursued further training and licensing to continue to work effectively with the mentally ill. My husband used to tease me that I have the whole alphabet after my name: MSW, LSW, ACSW, LCSW.

I learned that success in therapy is based on the relationship between the therapist and the client. I developed the skills to tune in, with warmth and empathy, during the therapeutic alliance with clients/patients. I was heartened to see that most of my patients, especially Filipinos, readily trusted and confided in me.

Reflecting back, my Filipino values of pakikisama (smooth inter-personal relations) and pakikiramdam (empathy) enabled me to create a friendly, supportive and trusting counseling environment. I served as a confidant, a sounding board, more like a supportive friend, a "go-between" and a peacemaker to husband and wife, parent and child, patching relationships torn apart by the many challenges of life.

My alphabet soup of licenses has been well used.

A SOCIAL WORKER'S
MENTAL HEALTH ADVICE

1. Smile and hum every morning as you wake up and continue throughout the day. It will keep you relaxed and less stressed.
2. Be grateful. Before I go to bed, I thank God for the little and big miracles that happened during the day.
3. Harness the power of your mind. We have the choice to think more positively and choose thoughts to make us feel better and act with less negative consequences.
4. Exercise. I walk in nature, stretch, dance.
5. Sleep well and eat nutritious meals. Our Filipino diet, plantation style with plenty of vegetables and little meat, is healthy.
6. Research the seven gifts of the Holy Spirit: knowledge, wisdom, understanding, courage/fortitude, counsel/discernment, knowledge, and fear of the Lord.. They will help you as it's helped me.
7. Laugh. We can smile and laugh ourselves out of depression and clear our minds to work on solutions. It's infectious and it's free.
8. Socialize!

With her MSW from UH Manoa, **Conchita Schlemmer** *served in three major Hawai'i state agencies: the Department of Human Services (DHS), North Foster Care; State Judiciary, Family Crises Services Family Court; Department of Health (DOH) Mental Health division. Family Guidance Center. She also worked as a clinician in private practice. She was a former member of the Behavioral Mental Health Concentration Advisory Council, and co-founded the Association of Filipino Social Workers of Hawai'i. Through supervision and certification, she has helped fellow social workers get their clinical social work licenses.*

Four

GEMISCHTER SATZ

A Blend of Three Flavors

by Maria Lourdes Soto Reininger

A dream of a white swan that filled the horizon when I was 14 was, according to my father, an omen of great happiness that was to come. What we did not know then, was that I was destined for Austria, a land of lakes and swans, a place which could hold great happiness, but like a treasure, had to be searched for, worked for, and finally find.

I was introduced to the Austrian gemischter satz in a wine tavern years ago. A gemischter satz is wine produced from a blend of many sorts of grapes. Gradually, this blend of undefined flavors became my favorite, perhaps because I identify myself with it. I can no longer identify myself as Filipina, pro-American, or European. I have become a gemischter satz, a unique blend of three worlds.

Austria is a beautiful but formidable place for a Filipina migrant. At the surface, it is a land of culture, beauty, music, inventors, a melting pot of European peoples, located in middle Europe. This impression is almost deceivingly simple, but at a closer look, Austria has been a witness to wars, prejudice, racism, occupation by the World War II victors, the rise and fall of aristocracy and an empire—a colorful but in many ways, a tragic, history. Is it any wonder then, that it is in Austria that the Freudian school of thought saw its birth? Since 1955, when then Chancellor Leopold Figl announced that Austria is free

("Österreich ist frei"), Austria has succeeded in rebuilding this country to one of the most stable and highest contributors to the European Union. It has successfully provided its citizens with a high quality of life, social security, health insurance, enviable medical standards and institutions, higher education incentives, a reliable retirement system, excellent transportation systems, and relatively low criminality. For years, it has pursued community beautification through planting more trees and greenery, subsidizing farmers and agriculture, and using alternative forms of energy rather than fossil fuel.

Arriving in 1976, I did not intend to carry over Filipino traditions in my new homeland. I was rather intent on learning the German language, a tool to enable me to integrate into this strange culture. I arrived at the time in Austrian history when the country was at a crossroads between racism and internationalism, 60 years after the end of the 650-year-old monarchy, and barely 30 years after the Second World War and the racial Nazi regime. Unknowingly, I was facing the greatest adventure of my life, a finishing school which would never end, a roller-coaster ride that would span more than 46 years.

Growing up in a typically large Filipino family whose first language was English, I did not speak the national language, Tagalog, until I was seven, which served me well in my education, as English was the language of instruction at that time. I spent my elementary and high school years with the German and Filipino nuns of the Benedictine order. I am forever grateful to the sisters of St. Scholastica's College in Manila for inculcating in me piety and discipline, in short, "ora et labora," and to my parents, who sent me there in my formative years. This would serve as an anchor during my college years in the secular world of the University of the Philippines.

Because of the educational revival brought about by the American occupation of the Philippines, my early background was pro-American. I realized only a few years later that there was more to the world than the USA. In college, I became a member of the University of the Philippines Student Catholic Action (UPSCA), a haven which lessened the shock of new surroundings and new beliefs and ideas, where I met like-minded students, a few of them becoming lifelong friends.

After my graduation in 1971, I chose to work with Philippine Airlines for its travel privileges. After a few years, I decided to pursue my master's' degree in Chicago, sponsored by an aunt who had become an American citizen. These plans were interrupted when I met a Viennese, whom I would marry after a whirlwind courtship and who would bring me to Austria.

Because I was able to travel the world courtesy of my airline privileges—from the Philippines to Southeast Asia, Europe, and the United States—I won many foreign friends and became familiar with numerous cultures. But these would hardly be adequate preparation for the enormous challenges that awaited me in Austria. A convent-bred girl in my early twenties with only my Catholic faith, my Filipino grit that I had inherited from my mother, and my steely determination to survive, I was transplanted into a totally unfamiliar culture.

I missed my big Filipino family in Manila, our festivities, the security of a large brood, the warm hospitality that seemed to have been ingrained in our race. I longed for the day when I would be able to have a satisfying argument in German, which appeared to be the entry to happiness and success in Austria. I found comfort and security in the familiar sound of church bells. It seemed that Austria had Catholic churches in every corner so I could visit and participate in Holy Mass. This was particularly important, as having given birth to my son and not working, isolation and loneliness threatened to rule my life.

I was neither a nurse nor an employee of the United Nations like most Filipino-Austrians in Vienna at that time. I rather was on my own. Gradually, I met other Filipino-Austrians from the Philippine Embassy, nurses and employees in the health sector and United Nations, and at church. The wife of an U.N.

diplomat whom I had befriended, advised me to get a baby sitter. Like many pioneers who had arrived in Austria in the 1970s, I did not need a nanny but a friend. Soon I was able to bring my only son to attend kindergarten. Conscious that my son was half Austrian and half Filipino, after he reached school age, I enrolled him at the Vienna International School to give him the opportunity to understand and become confident in being multi-national. This has proven to be the right decision as, thankfully, he is a well-balanced citizen, family man, husband and father, secure in his identity of being half Austrian and half Filipino (but more Austrian).

It was providential that I garnered my first job in Vienna with Trans World Airlines. When TWA folded, I was hired by the U.S. Embassy in Vienna to open its future Information Systems Center. This offered me a rewarding career, where I was a pioneer in implementing the swift technological advancements over a span of 30 years.

The Filipino community of Vienna started in the 1970s with the arrival of the first health workers and nurses. At present, the first, second, and third-generation Filipino-Austrians number approximately 30,000 (source: Statistics, Philippine Embassy in Vienna 2020). They bring Filipino festivals to Austria, like the Sinulog, the Barrio Fiesta, the Philippine Independence Day Ball, and the Penafrancia Fluvial Procession. It is not the largest migrant group in Austria, but it is one of the most active.

There are about 54 recorded Filipino organizations, mostly regional, professional, or faith-based, with a number having organized themselves under an umbrella organization. The Filipinos in Austria rarely or never are in the news for breaking the law or even for small misdemeanors. Filipinos are known to be religious, peaceful, music-loving, and hospitable. Most are employed in hospitality and food service agencies, health sectors, and the retail trade. They are very well represented in the United Nations headquarters in Vienna.

There are three landmarks in my involvement in the Filipino community.

First, together with a group of about 25 Filipinas, I spearheaded the founding of Babaylan Austria in 1994, and became its first chairwoman. Babaylan Austria evolved from the existing Pilipina Sa Austria, a small group of women who had mainly concentrated on helping fellow Filipinas in dire need of support; for example, women who worked as maids and who were abused in various ways but could not leave their place of work because their passports were taken away by the employers. The concept behind the founding of Babaylan Austria went further. It extended its activities by offering education as a means of empowerment. We organized seminars, self-defense sessions, awareness sessions, and had fun with dancing and being together. Friendships were formed and bonds were strengthened.

I had envisioned an organization that would cater to the needs of Filipino women in Austria. It was beneficial to be networked with the European Babaylan, but the Austrian Babaylan was conceived to be completely autonomous, as the needs in Austria were different. When I attended a meeting called by Babaylan Europe in Paris in the early 1990s, I met delegates from Germany, Netherlands, Spain, France, and Italy. It was interesting to observe that although all of us were Filipinas, the outward character and way of speaking of each delegate had been influenced by the country of origin.

Back in Vienna, at a meeting held in the traditional Café Landtmann, we validated and signed the constitution of Babaylan Austria. Its main goal, in general terms, was to uplift the status of Filipino women. Not limited to assisting women in dire need of help, our club offered educational modules and information on Austrian culture and traditions, as well as social benefits to its membership, which gradually had increased to 35 to 40 Filipinas. The men in the Filipino community of the 1970s, an important factor in our work, also supported our efforts! My husband notably, was our ardent supporter.

To survive or send money for their old age to the Philippines or to support their needy relatives, many Filipinos in Austria resort to working part-time as housemaids in households. A few others are luckier and receive pension privileges from their employers. Periodically, I receive requests for assistance in finding a Filipino maid. I politely decline. It has at times been unpleasant; many requesters believe that they are doing us a favor offering this kind of employment to fellow Filipinos.

It is my belief that this chain of servitude, if possible, needs to be broken. I therefore welcome the news we received from high sources in the Philippine Embassy in Vienna, that Austria is now offering the Philippines entry into the work market for medical personnel, especially caregivers and nurses, of which Austria is in dire need.

At this time of writing, there has been a rise in crimes against women. Austria has never experienced such high statistics, probably due to the present pandemic lockdown. As one of the pioneers working for the betterment of conditions of women among the Filipino migrants, I am glad that our work in the 1990s has proven to be significant, especially for our early migrants who were looking to strengthen financial and personal status, identity, and leadership at that point in time.

The second landmark came after I was elected to be the chairperson of the Core Committee for Philippine Centennial Celebrations in Austria from 1996 to1999. I call this period the "Golden Age of Filipino-Austrians." Then Ambassador of the Philippines Jose F. Zaide had called upon the Filipino-Austrian community to support the Philippine Centennial Celebrations which originated in the Philippines. As head of the Core Committee, I travelled to the westernmost provinces of Austria accompanied by my husband and some co-supporters. We were met by Filipino community leaders with enthusiasm and euphoria, mixed with a sense of pride, patriotism, and longing for their motherland.

Two notable activities were a month-long showing of Filipino movies, and an extravagant and successful fashion show that highlighted Filipino designers and their creations, presented by carefully chosen Filipinas in the community. The top fundraising activity was the Ball at Vienna's Rathaus (City Hall). I formed committees, negotiated with city and government agencies responsible for security, and Rathaus authorities. Attended by about 3,500 guests, the Ball was a memorable culmination of months of fundraising and publicity work. When then President of the Philippines Fidel Ramos arrived in Vienna, about 2,000 Filipino Austrians greeted him at the Hotel Hilton, led by Ambassador Zaide.

Speaking in German, Tagalog, and English, I welcomed the President, his wife, and his entourage of cabinet officers, business leaders, and ministers. I smile when recalling what President Ramos said to me at the end of my speech. "Malou, you can be a senator of the Philippines," he said. Upon hearing this, my best friend quipped, "and I will be your public relations head!" I was surprised at the President's political savvy!

The presidential visit ended with a presentation of a check which represented a hefty contribution to the Centennial Celebrations in the Philippines. This was the climax of a fascinating period in the history of the Filipino community in Austria.

A few months later, the core committee decided to document the Centennial activities by investing some of the funds generated by the Ball to publishing a book. After months of work, the book "Celebration" was presented at a gala evening held at the National Museum. It documents almost two years of Philippine Centennial activities in Austria.

The remaining funds amounting to what today would be approximately €10,000 were donated to the Children's Ward of the Philippine General Hospital. Only 20 years after the first Filipino migrants arrived in the country, the community showed

Flower laying ceremony at the Vienna Rathaus spearheaded by Malou (center) and members of the Filipino-Austrian community.

success and unity. I believe this was the turning point in the history of Filipino migration in Austria. It was a coming-out party of sorts.

The story of the Centennial celebrations would not be complete without mentioning the planting of a catalpa tree in front of the Vienna Rathaus (City Hall) on June 5, 1998. To acknowledge the sacrifices and achievements of the first Filipino migrants and succeeding generations who have planted their roots in this country, I thought of a sustainable event that would remain for decades to come. After I had approached city officials, we became the first migrant group to receive permission to plant a tree on the city hall grounds. The city donated a catalpa tree as well (trompeten baum or trumpet tree).

The first tree-planting ceremony was held at the Rathaus Park with much fanfare. The ceremony, attended by about 200 Filipino-Austrians and Austrian guests, was led by Vienna's

Mayor-Governor Dr. Michael Häupl and Ambassador Jose Zaide. Assurances of friendship of the two countries were shared. A twin catalpa tree was planted too, just in case the first one did not survive.

These two trees have now become a symbol of friendship of the host country, Austria, and the Philippines. On Philippine Independence Day in 2018, 20 years after the planting of the catalpa tree, the Philippine-Austrian Cultural and Educational Society (PACES) revived the tradition and spearheaded the flower laying ceremony. The flower-laying tradition has continued. On June 12, 2020, Mayor-Governor of Vienna Dr. Michael Ludwig together with Philippine Ambassador to Austria Maria Cleofe Natividad led the guests at second flower laying ceremony organized by PACES with an enthusiastic, patriotic, flag-bearing Filipino-Austrian crowd. In June 2021, despite the pandemic lockdown, there was even a larger crowd and participation.

The third landmark that led to my involvement with the Philippine community was the founding of PACES. The former Philippine Ambassador to Austria, Zeneida Collinson-Angara was behind the forming of an organization that would support science students in the Philippines. In 2016, I was invited to join the core group of like-minded persons that founded PACES. I was vice president 2017-2018, and from 2018 thru 2020, I was president of this organization. Presently, I am a member of PACES' Scholarship Committee.

PACES members and supporters believe that the key to Philippines' progress is through science and technology. Since its founding, PACES has sponsored a series of live and videoconferencing informative lectures on scientific subjects, like Peaceful Uses of Atomic Energy; Volcanology, Earthquake and Typhoon Warning Systems; Science in Management ("My Boss is an Algorithm"), and the Uses and Misuses of Statistics. PACES supports talented and financially needy STEM (Science, Technology, Engineering, Mathematics) university students with scholarships that include living expenses and digital tools necessary for graduation. In return, scholars are obliged to work in the Philippines after graduation, corresponding to the number of scholarship years.

One of the PACES scholars is now a computer engineer, and presently holds a job in a computer firm in Manila. A second scholar, a graduate of Mindanao State University in Iligan City, passed the Board examinations. He is now a certified metallurgical engineer. Our first two female scholars, from Batangas and Cagayan, also passed their Board examinations and are now certified civil engineers. In 2021, PACES awarded university scholarships to four students from Luzon, one of them taking an engineering course, one taking up Industrial Technology, and two majoring in computer science technology.

As diverse groups increasingly enter Austria, more awareness of integration and racism issues have become needed in this country. I am grateful that I was never a victim of an openly demonstrated racism or prejudice. Perhaps I was oblivious to its many signs as I was busy with career and family, or I was living in a sheltered environment. I was once told that I was never a victim because I was beautiful. True or not, there still exists a covert prejudice, which is present in many modern, mixed societies. Once I recognized this fact, I never succumbed to the luxury of self-pity. In reply to a question whether I ever experienced racism, my attitude has always been, that if ever I would be rejected because of my race, the person who rejects me is the loser, not vice-versa. I am happy to have this understanding that has helped me enjoy life in Austria.

Austria's history is rich and complicated. It is in Middle Europe, was once the center of the Habsburg empire, and a hub of various ethnic groups with their own religious beliefs, culture, and traditions. Austria, however, has also had a history of racism, notably against Jews and other minorities. It is said that having lost its empire and experienced a ten-year occupation by the World War II victors, a native Austrian has become resentful of anyone or any group that threatens his existence. The situation is presently made more complicated due to issues of illegal migration, which has reached its peak in the last five years.

In 2015, I was appointed Integration Ambassador under the auspices of the Austrian Ministry of European, Foreign and Integration Affairs. I accepted this appointment as a tool in assisting the integration of Filipino migrants and their families in Austria. Integration is a lengthy process, involving a spirit of willingness to learn and be a productive member of the adopted country. It does not mean complete assimilation but a flexibility to live according to the customs and traditions of the new homeland. It starts with learning the language and is a never-ending adaptation.

Simple customs, like for example, the use of a fork and knife instead of a fork and spoon, need to be learned. When entering a building or a gathering, one greets with a simple "Grüß Gott" (from "Gott grüße Dich" or "God bless"). The use of the third person "sie" as a sign of respect is not very different from our Filipino custom of "po" or "ho" when speaking to an older person or someone higher in authority. However, it is more formal and must be agreed upon by both parties before the familiar "du" or "you" is used. The older of the two persons, or the one with higher position or authority has to propose the use of the familiar "du."

Every province, partly due to the occupation by the four World War II Allies, has its own particular customs and traditions. Every province has its own design for the dirndl, the native dress used in formal gatherings, balls, and other festivities. Easter is celebrated among devoted Christians more significantly than Christmas. It is usually a time for gift-giving, although Christmas comes as second, when family reunions are held.

Most Filipinos prefer serving in abundance, buffet style, placing the various dishes on a sideboard or on a large dinner table. In many Austrian homes, each dish is usually served in the order they are eaten with the hostess serving a portion for each person on the table. In Austria, social services have taken the place of the family as a support system. The elderly or sick are placed in nursing homes or hospices, especially if there is no one to take care of them. Filipinos traditionally prefer to keep their elderly at home and care for them for as long as possible.

I have left my country of birth, but I was never really gone. I still carry with me the traditions, quirks, characteristics, language, food, love of children and elderly, love of God and family, and a joy that seems to be inborn. My late grandmother in her simple, deep wisdom said to my Austrian husband, "We (Filipinos) are poor but happy."

My husband is a true-blue Viennese who also comes from a large family like I do. We live in typical Filipino-Austrian fashion, celebrating special occasions like birthdays, with food and cooking. Our lives are a mix of both worlds. I like cooking Filipino food, especially the lumpiang shanghai that I make for my grandchild. She vows that although she has tasted many others, mine are the best!

My husband and I are active in our parish and are involved in community politics, perhaps more than the typical Filipino-Austrian. My husband has supported me in my work within the Filipino community through all these years. Like many Filipino-Austrian families, religion and Christian worship play a huge part in our daily lives. We go to an Austrian parish, the Augustinerkirche, well-known and visited by tourists and locals alike for the sacred music by Augustinerkirche Chor and orchestra during Sunday German high masses. For a time, we sang with the Augustinerkirche Chor. It was a joyful experience and a dream come true to be able to sing sacral music like Wolfgang Amadeus Mozart's "Krönungsmesse" with a professional orchestra and choir. Having sung with the U.P. Concert Chorus in my college days, I look back with gratefulness at my parents for encouraging music and my artistic development through piano lessons when I was a child.

My husband and I also belong to a bible study group that has an international membership from about 25 countries. It evolved from the Vienna English-speaking Catholic community, led by Professor Dr. Cyril Desbruslais. SJ, from Pune, India. For many Filipinos in Austria, the church, their parish, is "home away from home." My fellow Filipinos gather after Holy Mass and each family brings a dish or whatever they can afford to share. Filipinos love to share a meal and socialize! Secularization is creeping into society. Many first- and second-generation Filipinos are worried that their children and grandchildren are no longer churchgoers. On a positive note, however, the Filipino parishes are still full of Fil-Austrian churchgoers.

What I would like to carry with me in Austria is the respect and love for elderly, love of family, and the spirit of helpfulness for those in need (bayanihan) or less fortunate. I would like children to respect their parents, and to kiss the hands of their grandparents. I recall those days when my parents would lead us in praying the rosary in the evenings during the month of May, and we would kiss our parents and siblings thereafter. I also recall kissing the hands of our grandparents, and they would bless us with a sign of the cross, a blessing that vaguely sounded like "Estibusanto" (Espiritu Santo or Holy Spirit). Our children and my siblings' children have long established their own families, but our families still cultivate close contact with each other.

I love Austria, but there is always a deep sense of longing for homeland and family left behind. Many Filipinos in diaspora are a unique blend of east and west. I often wonder what our mission in the world is, what role our history and culture, both native and adopted, play in our lives.

In the adopted country, each edifice, whether it be a castle, a church, a wall or a palace, has a story to tell. The Philippines has churches that tell stories of the Spanish colonial time, our religious customs mostly originating from that period. The Catholic schools in the Philippines remind me of the first foreign missionaries who established schools that have flourished and developed into colleges or universities. Intramuros in Manila speaks of the torture of those who dared fight for freedom from foreign oppressors. Non-sectarian schools and universities like the University of the Philippines or Siliman University in Dumaguete City, remind one of the influences of American occupation and education.

Many of us have memories of summer vacations spent in wooden houses in the provinces of our ancestors, maybe even with a sparkling clean brook behind the house. Each beach, each mountain road that curbs dangerously until one reaches his or her destination has a personal meaning.

My unspectacular story ends here for the present. Austria is so much different now than when I arrived more than 40 years ago. Filipinos are recognized as Filipinos and no longer as Chinese or Thai or Japanese or Korean. There is a strong move towards integration of migrants, more opportunities and jobs for non-native born Filipino-Austrians, and more respect for their achievements, talents, and contributions to society than before. The Filipino community in Austria is doing a good job of preserving our valuable cultural practices and traditions. My perception is derived from the activities of the number of regional and non-regional clubs that have sprouted through the years and their many cultural presentations and events.

The migration that escalated in the 1970s due to the economic and reprisal conditions then in our country is irreversible. Through the years, I managed to keep my Filipino identity, while enriching myself with adopting a new one, ending up as a blend of three cultures. I believe that the Filipino soul and its sensitivity has much to contribute to this country, as well as to the universality of mankind. However, in doing so, we should not give up our identity which has emerged from centuries of evolution and development.

 *Born in post-war Manila, **Maria Lourdes (Malou) Soto Reininger** is a product of western-oriented, religious schooling by Benedictine convent nuns, and secular, western-oriented education at the University of the Philippines in Diliman, Quezon City, and Webster University in Vienna. Since 1976, she has since made Vienna her home while participating in the swift, fascinating developments in computer science technology in Europe. Married to a Viennese who had an international career, she is a Filipino-Austrian community leader whose social- philanthropic activities have resulted from her belief that "there is no faith without good works." A few months after this writing, Malou lost her beloved husband Irmfried after a lingering illness.*

Five

LIKE A SWAYING BAMBOO

My Acculturation as a Filipina Nurse

by Lilia Ponce Manangan

I first heard of acculturation, the process of learning and incorporating the values, beliefs, customs, language in a new environment, from Arnold "Arnulfo," my husband, when I met him in Hawai'i in 1973. I was a new immigrant, just graduated from Saint Paul College of Nursing in Manila, Philippines. Hawai'i was a new world: new culture, people, behaviors, language, way of thinking, talking; even some people have that distinct way of moving and swaying their bodies. I immersed myself into this adventure. Excited! Exhilarated yet uncertain. Confident yet insecure.

Perhaps, my acculturation into America required the resilience of the swaying bamboo with its ability to withstand even the strongest wind. Go with the flow. Bend. Smile. Do your best. Bend again. Solve. Act. Save. Heal. Listen. Embrace. Sway with the wind.

I have fond memories of the small barrio where I was born and grew up in Maasasin, Magsingal, Ilocos Sur, Philippines. It is in a lush valley bordered by the Cordillera mountains in the east. It is where my paternal grandfather bought land with money he earned as a sakada (plantation worker) in Hawai'i. It is where our Ponce family (uncles, auntie, and cousins) lived off the land. A river cascaded through that valley along the edge of the mountain. During rainy season that river was impassable due to the strong raging muddy water. I remember being scared watching the roaring river dislodging portions of the river banks and whatever was on its path. However, when the river was calmer after the rainy season we would catch small shrimp, crabs, and fish. I felt carefree just playing around in the clear water.

I was happy running through the rice fields, hunting for mushrooms, edible fruits, and bamboo shoots in the forest. My cousins and I used to climb trees picking ripe fruits: caimito or star apple, guava, pomelo, jackfruit, tamarind, sarguelas or Spanish plum, lomboy or Java plum, tiesa or egg fruit, and mango. As kids we would pick ripe bananas and papayas with long sticks and eat them right there and then. Then we would help our parents plant and harvest the crops. Our family and other close relatives lived close to one another, so it was customary to take turns helping each family during the planting and harvesting season. It is that sense of togetherness and living off the land that I miss.

Our town in Magsingal had a municipal plaza where special events were held right next to the oldest and biggest building-the century-old Catholic church. We also had a tiendaan (market) where we could buy a variety of items- clothing, vegetables, fruits, fish, and freshly butchered meats. There were also sari-sari (variety) stores, bakery, and other small stands.

Our barrio's elementary school ended at the fourth grade. So, my parents let me live with my unmarried aunt and widowed grandmother in town, miles away, to attend fifth grade. The town school was so much bigger and my teachers and classmates were so different from our barrio school. I remember my teacher asking me in a not-so-kind way why I was always smiling. I did not know why because it was just how my natural face looked. I did not feel welcomed in that bigger school so I was happy when I went back to our barrio school because the officials decided to add fifth and sixth grades. I was one of the first graduates and my parents were happy that I was the valedictorian.

I attended Saint William's Institute, a Catholic high school annexed to the church in town and administered by nuns of the sisters of Saint Paul. I was excited and proud to wear the required Paulinian uniform. I took my schooling seriously because I knew my parents were working hard for my tuition. Also, I had to live up to high expectations by our teachers because our class had six of us valedictorians from various elementary schools. I enjoyed being there and I am forever thankful for the love and support of my parents. I showed my gratitude by graduating with honors.

Our high school principal encouraged me and one of my good friends, a female classmate, to attend Saint Paul College of Nursing in Manila, a big city college, well known for attracting the wealthy. Our relatives in Manila discouraged my parents to send me there because they knew it was very expensive. They knew we were farmers from a barrio. But with great determination and faith, my parents sent me to Saint Paul College of Manila. This was a big adjustment on my part. Mingling with my rich fellow students and maneuvering the intricacies of living in the big city of Manila were challenging.

Fortunately, with the grace of God, my parents were able to immigrate to Hawai'i because my mother had a U.S. birth certificate. My maternal grandparents, who were also previous plantation workers in Hawai'i, went back to the Philippines for vacation, when my mother was a baby. However, my grandparents were not able to go back to Hawai'i because while vacationing in the Philippines, my grandfather died from a logging accident. My mother grew up in the Philippines not aware that she was a U.S. citizen until someone told my dad that his wife was born in Hawai'i.

So, my mother who was pregnant with my youngest brother travelled to Hawai'i and stayed with my uncle and family in a plantation home in Kahuku. My father and my siblings followed thereafter. I remained in Manila to finish my Bachelor of Science in Nursing degree at Saint Paul College.

My initial reaction was "Is this Hawai'i?" when we drove out of the Honolulu airport. Waipahu, where my parents lived, looked more like our province in the Philippines. Same weather, same people, same language, same marungay (moringa), papaya, mango, guava, coconut trees. But I was happy to be reunited finally with my parents and six siblings after so many years.

My first job was as a paid volunteer graduate nurse of Volunteers in Service for America (VISTA) assigned to the Lanakila Health Center, a tuberculosis clinic in Honolulu. My onsite supervisor and fellow nurses were mostly Japanese. I had some trepidation about working with them because my father had told us stories of atrocities by Japanese soldiers during WWII. However, my co-workers supported and accepted me. I felt comfortable working with them and enjoyed my job.

My second job was as a staff charge/registered nurse at the then-Saint Francis Hospital in Honolulu. The director of nursing who I think was part Chinese-Portuguese-Hawaiian, interviewed me and asked why I spoke good English. She told me that they were taking a big risk in hiring me because it was their first time to hire an RN graduate from the Philippines. She hired two of us Filipina RNs that year and after proving that we could do the job, many more were hired afterwards.

It was challenging to work at the hospital as a young nurse especially when my patients thought I looked just like a high school kid. I remember being overwhelmed with the new equipment, instruments, and medical terminologies. I felt exhausted caring for cancer patients especially when they died and I was the shift charge nurse. But I was able to take courses during the day for my master's of Public Health at the University of Hawai'i, Manoa.

I met my husband Arnold at a VISTA party at the house of the Filipina medical doctor from the Hawai'i Department of Health. I was so enthralled with Arnold's nice soothing voice, his Americanized way of speaking English, and his intelligent conversation. He helped me learn the local Hawaiian lifestyle and introduced me to his Americanized Filipino friends. Most of them were from the University of Hawai'i and were involved with Operation Manong, a group dedicated to the betterment of Filipino students. Arnold was a community worker who helped newly arrived immigrants acculturate to the U.S. lifestyle. We got married and had a two-year-old son when we moved, with our master's of Public Health credentials to Roosevelt, Utah.

It was March 1979 when we first stepped into the snow country of the West. I had to ask Arnold to stop the car on the side of the road so I could touch snow for the first time in my life. I will always remember that exciting moment, feeling the snowflakes as they dropped on the white covered ground. We were driving my rear-wheel drive Ford Mustang II and when we stopped at a gas station, the attendant was shocked when he saw our Hawai'i license plate, "Are you crazy? Coming here all the way from Hawai'i?" Yes, we were crazy. But we liked our adventure: living and working with the Native Americans in Fort Duchesne and Roosevelt, Utah, about two-and-a-half hour drive east of Salt Lake City.

Arnold was first assigned to the U.S. Indian Health Service Center. I did not know what was in store for us but I was excited in this new Wild West country. We just read the new book on the power of positive thinking towards prosperity in mind, body, and soul that my cousin and his wife gave us as a farewell gift. The Divine Providence that this book emphasized gave us the impetus to be positive in our new experiences. It helped us be at peace with people around us.

I was offered a part-time job as an instructor at a nursing school for licensed practical nurses. I was hesitant at first because I did not plan on being a teacher. I took the challenge nevertheless. My students were white females and older than me but I felt accepted as their teacher. I enjoyed teaching them gerontological nursing which was one of my major studies in my master's degree in Public Health.

Arnold and I decided to buy a brand new Volkswagen camper van because we wanted to experience camping and fishing in the abundant mountain lakes. Our second son was born in Roosevelt, Utah and so we had two young boys to go fishing and camping with. We would go on long weekend fishing trips in the remote mountain lakes and bring home rainbow trout that filled our newly bought freezer. We would bring a cooler full of those frozen trout to Hawai'i or California whenever we visited our relatives.

We were happy to belong to the small staff: physicians, dentist, nurses, psychologist, laboratorian. Most were from different states such as Alaska, Illinois, North Dakota. It was exciting to experience the diversity of cultures for the first time within a predominantly Mormon population. I learned from our Mormon neighbor to preserve vegetables and fish by processing them in a big canning pressure cooker. I also learned to make jams and jellies and bake apple pies for church bake sales. We got along well with our Mormon friends. Yes, some tried to convert us but they saw us devoutly attending mass and involved in programs at our small Catholic church.

Arnold came home one day with an International Travel-All, supposedly all-terrain truck with the U.S. Forest Service sticker barely visible on it. He told me that the auctioneer was talking so fast and Arnold, being his first time in an auction, raised his hand at $750 and the auctioneer said, "Sold!"

When we moved to Southwest Colorado, we drove that old Travel-All truck, loaded with a 1,000-pound steel/brick wood stove fireplace built by the Mormons in Utah. It was a very efficient heating stove with space for cooking and grilling. We had to ask six of our co-workers and newly found friends to help us carry that woodstove into the house. Every summer, armed with a chain saw that sometimes did not work, we cut and chopped truckloads of wood from the mountains for the winter months. What a great way to exercise and keep our bodies active and functioning. I remember how our two boys would help out as much as they could and roam around the forest as we cut and loaded the wood into the Travel-All.

We initially lived in a home owned by the Bureau of Indian Affairs in the Southern Ute Indian reservation in Ignacio, Colorado. One of our neighbors was a member of the Southern Ute tribe married to one of my coworkers, a member of the Chippewa tribe in Minnesota. She gave us a recipe of her famous rum cake that I still bake to this day. We loved the frozen walleye filets from Minnesota that she used to give us. We stayed at their home in Ignacio whenever we went back to ski downhill in Durango.

My first job in Colorado was as a public home healthcare nurse for the San Juan Basin County Health Department in Durango. I had to learn to drive a standard car to drive the county-issued car. I drove through gravel county roads to get to some of my patients' homes. The only traffic involved cows or sheep being herded to pasture by ranchers.

Our home was on a roughly three-acre lot, of which a large portion was pasture. We took on raising cows, sheep, goats, chickens; not the best decision in life to blindly become pseudo farmers. It would take another chapter to describe the hard farm work with only Arnold, myself, and our two young boys who promised to help, only to say too tired when it was time to do chores.

Then I got a fulltime clinical nursing position at the Southern Ute Health Center in Ignacio just a 15-minute drive from our home in Bayfield, which was ten minutes from Durango. My patients used to ask me, "What tribe do you belong to?" I would answer, "The overseas Filipino tribe." They said I looked like one of the Pueblo Native Americans in New Mexico and Arnold looked like a Navajo. We enjoyed getting to know the Native Americans and even danced at powwows and bear dances. They gave us a traditional outfit and wool blanket when we bid them farewell to move to Georgia.

We moved from Colorado in our Volkswagen camper van filled with indoor plants to Georgia during the wintry days of 1989. We had to drive very slowly because the Siberian Express snowstorm was ahead of us. We were happy to see that our plants survived the freezing temperature, and we were awed at the sight of all the trees when we finally arrived at our new home in Stone Mountain, Georgia.

Lilia and Arnold in his uniform as US Public Health Service Commissioned Corp., Stone Mountain, Georgia.

Arnold secured a job as a health services officer and I as a technical information specialist at the Hospital Infections Program at the Centers for Disease Control and Prevention (CDC) in Atlanta. It was a blessing that Arnold and I got a job with CDC. It was a lateral move for both of us but we knew this would provide more opportunities for advancement. Also, it is a bigger city ideal for our two boys' life and learning exposure.

It was at the height of the AIDS/HIV epidemic and my main job was to answer questions on infection control in hospital settings. Every day, the physician on call and I would answer questions from physicians and nurses or other healthcare professionals about the possibility of transmitting HIV from accidents involving needle sticks used in HIV patients.

Once again, I had to learn fast. I answered letters from all over the world and have collected the stamps from those countries. After a few years, I realized that I needed to take the initiative to get into a higher-level position.

I took on more difficult research projects on infection control. I published my research findings in peer-reviewed scientific journals. I requested our personnel office to reclassify my position and after a few years and three audits, I was classified as an epidemiologist. With the promotion came bigger responsibilities along with some unsupportive supervisors. I felt stressed especially when I had to juggle between my job and my responsibilities: taking care of our boys and my elderly parents who were far away in Hawai'i. Despite these challenges, I was motivated to do my best.

My work took me all over the USA, Canada, Guam, Mexico, South Africa, Philippines, Vietnam, and the Pacific Islands. I gave scientific presentations and investigated severe adverse outcomes from medications used to prevent tuberculosis. I enjoyed the opportunities of publishing, traveling, and teaching healthcare professionals across the USA and the world. Being a CDC epidemiologist was most fulfilling.

Living in Georgia allowed us as a family to be exposed and blend in with the Blacks, Caucasians, and other racial groups. Atlanta is a cosmopolitan city. We befriended people from East India, China, Japan, Korea, Peru, and Europe. Arnold goes to get his haircut at a salon owned by a Vietnamese. Arnold and I immersed ourselves with the southern culture of hospitality. Our Caucasian daughter-in-law and her family being native Georgians have that hospitable lifestyle. I'm all smiles when our in-laws greet us with "hey, y'all" in their southern accent.

We also started a hospitality business by acquiring vacation rental homes in Georgia, North Carolina, and South Carolina through the years. We learned the world of Airbnb, Homeaway, and VRBO. It was a big challenge juggling managing our homes and our fulltime jobs. But despite the hard work, we are enjoying the fruits of our labor and we now pay a management company to do the work. We are both retired from our jobs at the CDC in Atlanta.

After living away from Hawai'i for more than 40 years, Arnold and I are completing the circle of life, back to where we came from. We now call Hawai'i home most of the time, because with the pandemic it hasn't been safe to travel back to Georgia where we still reside for part of the year. We were surprised to find that we needed to be acculturated again to the current culture and lifestyle of Hawai'i.

We are enjoying reconnecting with relatives and friends. We both have large extended families here because among our siblings, we were the only ones who relocated to the continental U.S. We find ourselves attending large family gatherings for events such as first-year birthdays, retirements, weddings, funerals, and holidays. These events have been unending and even tiring at times. We love the local food that we missed all these years and find ourselves overeating fatty but yummy local dishes. We have also tried hard to understand the local lingo, Pidgin, and have even relearned to speak it, mixed with Ilokano and English.

The pandemic is a mixed blessing. We are in touch in a different way. We learned to connect with family and friends using technology. It was so hard not to be able to visit my dad in the nursing home especially before he passed away. But at least we were able to be on Facetime, Zoom, and WEBEX with him. I always wanted to learn hula and I am excited to dance it many times a week through Zoom. We pray the rosary novena daily with fellow Filipina nurses via Zoom for everyone, especially for those who are affected by the pandemic. We also garden and walk and enjoy the all-year-round warm Hawai'i weather while taking care of my 92-year-old mom who is on hemodialysis and in a nursing home.

As I reflect on my journey as a granddaughter of sakada in Hawai'i and a daughter of a farmer from a small barrio in the Philippines, I feel proud of what I have accomplished. I look back to my childhood when I used to carry very heavy pots of food to the rice field helpers, take tobacco leaves to the smoke house for proper drying, and help my dad calculate the total cost of the dried tobacco leaves that he bought and sold to merchants in town. Then I became a Registered Nurse and worked in a variety of settings such as clinics, home healthcare, hospitals, nursing schools, topped off by my career as an epidemiologist (GS-14) at the world renowned, national public health agency, CDC.

I am at awe and grateful to the many who nurtured me to be who I am today. My mentors were parents, friends, teachers, co-workers and most importantly my husband. They all served as my inspiration and motivation to overcome challenges. They helped me become successful and resilient. More importantly, I could not have achieved my goals without the grace of the Lord.

My acculturation journey as a Filipina nurse in America has been an adventure and a blessing. Experiencing the variety of American landscapes from tropical forests and ocean to the Appalachian snow-capped mountains and lakes has been just amazing! Most especially, interacting with the diverse groups of people from different cultures has definitely enriched my life and that of my family. Like the swaying bamboo I learned to be resilient and trusting, to go where God is leading us. I am eager to find out what the future brings in our golden years!

 *For more than 40 years, **Lilia Ponce Manangan** worked as a Registered Nurse in various healthcare settings in Hawai'i, Utah, Colorado, and Georgia. She and her husband Arnold live in Hawai'i and Georgia. She enjoys traveling, gardening, and hula dancing. She thanks Arnold for his unwavering support and valuable insight in writing this article.*

Six

IN SEARCH OF A BETTER FUTURE

by Elizabeth Jocson

My full name is Elizabeth Aquino Siapno Jocson. My mom's surname is Aquino while my dad's surname was Siapno. My married name is Jocson.

My dad went to school to be an engineer and he got a job in Olongapo at the US Subic Naval Base. We lived in Caloocan, Metro-Manila in Bagong Barrio, a poor area close to Manila Central University. We lived in this small house—my mom and four kids (three daughters and a son).

My dad decided that he wanted to go to America. He didn't want his kids to grow up the way he did—very poor. He wanted something better for us. He was working at the shipyard, and since the ship he was working on was going to New York, he decided to be a stowaway. Yes, he was a stowaway on a US naval ship going to New York!

I was nine years old when my dad left in 1972. He knew he had relatives in California. But he didn't know his geography—that California was far away from New York. He just knew that those two places were in the United States.

I think $20 was the cost of the fare then for the trip on the Greyhound bus from New York to California. It took him three or four days on the bus and to get to West Covina to find the family members that he knew from Olongapo. He told them, "I'm your brother, your sister's husband. What do I need to do to get a job?"

In the 1970s, they were not strict about scrutinizing your paperwork to get a job. Because he was trained in mechanical engineering, his relatives said, "You know Boeing, the one that makes the airplanes? They are looking for shift workers." They got him a job there, the start of his working career. He's a smart guy and eventually got promoted to engineer.

In about a year or two, he asked, "How do I get my papers done so I can bring my family here?" Somebody told him, "Well, you have to marry somebody, but you're married in the Philippines, so you can't do that."

To solve that problem, he made my grandma convince my aunt to pretend that she was my mom that he would be divorcing. My aunt signed the divorce forms so he could marry a woman they found for him. She was an old maid working at the USC medical hospital as a nurse practitioner.

My dad said, "If I marry you, I'll pay you." But she ended up falling in love with him. She agreed to the arrangement so long as he really divorced his wife in the Philippines. So he did. My mom had no idea what was going on. But within two years of marrying that nurse-practitioner, he got his green card.

When he got his green card, he said, "I'm going back to the Philippines because I have a son in the Philippines with my ex-wife." But he didn't tell her that, yes, I do have a son, but I also have three girls. So he went back to the Philippines and told my mom that he wanted to bring his kids to California. My mom refused but my dad was insistent. "It is not about you and me anymore. You want them to have a better future. And once they get to America, we can get together again as a family," he assured her.

When we arrived in California in April of 1978, my stepmother threw a big party. She invited all the Filipinos in the neighborhood and all the nurses that she knew. She wanted everybody to meet the handsome man she married and fell in love with, and tell them that she was going to have a son.

Our flight got delayed and we didn't arrive until midnight, so the party was over when we arrived. When my dad picked us up, all four of us showed up. She looked at us and said, "I thought you said you have one son?"

From that point on, it became a classic stepmother-stepdaughter relationship. It was never nice. I guess my dad told my stepmother, Mercedes, that my mom was a bad person and that it was my grandma and my aunt who took care of us. That's why Mercedes mistreated us so badly because we came from a not-so-good mom. My mom and dad made many sacrifices. Their marriage suffered so we could have a better future.

The first thing that my stepmother said when we got up the next day was, "Well, you guys are pretty much old enough to go look for a job after school." We're like, "Wait a minute, we just got here."

Three days later, we were enrolled in an ESL (English as a Second Language) class. English is our third language. I speak Tagalog, Ilocano, and understand Pangasinan since my dad is from Pangasinan and my mom is from Nueva Ecija, a Tagalog-speaking province. Soon after, I got a job at Thrifty's.

I went straight to high school. I graduated sixth grade in the Philippines, but our new school here made us take a test; I passed it and was sent to ninth grade. I came here when I was 12 going on 13, and by 16, I was done with high school.

It was traumatic for us to move from the Philippines to California. In Caloocan, all we knew was that we had a dad who was somewhere working, but we never really got to know him well. When you're coming from poverty in the Philippines, your vision of America is San Francisco or New York. But Orange Grove in West Covina is the countryside, very rural, mostly mountains in the distance, no green grass, and very dry. We lived in a one-acre property and my dad had horses, rabbits, and ducks. We came to America to live in the province! Every weekend we went to the swap meet to sell fruits, lettuce, and whatever produce my dad grew in his garden. Instead of roller skating with the kids or hanging out with friends, we worked selling vegetable, fruits, even old clothes.

After school, we worked at a shop scooping ice cream; this didn't require us to talk since our English wasn't so good, and it was fun. We were getting paid $1.90 an hour back then. That was our pocket money. My dad said, "You each have to pay me $20 every month because you live with me." That's what my stepmother required. We tried to send money to my mom regularly. Every time we called our mom, Mercedes would say, "You have to pay for the long-distance fees." We paid for that, too.

After high school, I decided I wanted to join the Air Force. I wanted to see the world. I just didn't want to be stuck in the farm in West Covina. But my dad's like, "No, you you're going to be a nurse. If you became a nurse, you will be like your stepmother." Even though he had divorced her by that time, he still valued her achievements. But I wanted to do what I wanted to do.

I passed the test to get into the Air Force. I had to get a physical which was conducted very early in the morning. I told my dad I needed a car to drive to take the test. He said, "Go drive my jeep." But he didn't tell me that there was something wrong with the brakes. I crashed the jeep into a beauty salon through its glass windows. All around me were pieces of glass. The jeep was totaled. Thank God nothing happened to me.

I ended up going to a community college and took up cosmetology for two years. I eventually got a job at a hair salon in Pasadena, mostly catering to senior citizens. I used a lot of hot rollers and a lot of hair spray. I hated it so much.

So if being a nurse made my dad happy, I figured I might as well be one. I enrolled in the Pasadena City College nursing program. I had to participate in a live surgery where the patient needed to have her stomach stapled. I've never seen a big lady like that cut up. When I saw that, I'm like, "No, no, I can't do this!" I ended up working as a bank teller instead.

At City College, I became a member of the Filipiniana Club. The universities and community colleges in Southern California were starting to establish Filipino clubs. We had friendly competitions for best dancers, best DJs, the most participation at parties. Our group always won because we had a good president. We kept our culture alive. During every International Day, we did something fun, like perform a Filipino or Hawaiian dance. Except for the Covid years, those of us who are still alive get together every three years.

I was working at the processing center of a bank when a colleague set me up with, Jose, a club promoter. In the 1980s, some guys wore makeup because they think they're models, which Jose was—six feet one inch and very good looking, a print model for newspaper ads. But he was more interested in re-applying his make-up, so I told him, "Hey, I'm going to the bathroom," a subtle way of avoiding him. When I went back to the dance floor to get a drink (my date Jose never offered me a drink), the bartender asked a girl, "Hey, did you see Carlito? We haven't seen him in months. He's finally got a day off from work and he's here tonight."

When I went to another bathroom another girl was saying, "Oh my gosh, Carlito is here tonight and blah, blah, blah."

I thought to myself, this is second time I heard the name Carlito. I'm going to look for this guy. I wondered how he would look—would he be like Jose—tall and good looking but always in the bathroom fixing his make-up?

At the party, a guy named Mario told me, "I really want to dance with your friend, but she won't dance with me, unless you dance too. Why don't you dance with my friend, Carlito?"

The whole time we were dancing, Carlito was very nice, making small talk. He even offered drinks, but I made it clear I'm not interested. By then, my girlfriend says, "I'm going to get the car. Are You ready to go?"

I said yes, but I didn't know that she was going with Mario and make out in the car. So I'm waiting and waiting and waiting at the front lobby for her. It was winter—20 or 30 degrees and here I was wearing a bustier and mini skirt with a little jacket and a bolero hat. I was really cold.

And then Carlito came. "I have something for you in the car," he said.

I thought, "What if he has a gun in the car, and folks may think I'm buying illegal stuff in the parking lot." He opened the trunk and got a jacket for me! He was a real gentleman.

It was December 22. On December 24, he invited me over to his house and told his mom that he had a surprise for her—meaning he met a Filipina that he liked.

At that time, I already had a child. "That's okay, just bring the baby with you," he assured me. When I arrived at his house, his mom who opened the door. She looked at me and she looked at the baby, and said, "Oh my! I'm a grandma!"

I said, "No, you're not this baby's grandma," but Carlito said, "Just go with it."

When I had to leave for work on December 26, Carlito's mom, Mama Conchita, said, "You don't have to worry about leaving the baby with a babysitter. Just leave the baby here," she insisted.

So that's how I found my husband, Carlito. Since then, I never left that house in Fullerton for the next 32 years. When my baby grew up, he acquired dual citizenship so he could play in the Philippine basketball league.

My dad petitioned for all his siblings and my grandma. When they came to America, they took jobs at McDonald's and worked as meat packers or in grocery stores so they could send money to the Philippines and be able to bring more family members to the country. For us, it's family ties that bind. We do whatever is required to search for a better future for one's family.

Five years after we arrived, we got our green card. Five years later my older sister got her citizenship and she petitioned for our mom to come to America. The immigration officials asked, "How would you support your mother here?" We four siblings all got together, pooled our money, and deposited it in her savings account. It took another ten years before we could see our mom again.

I have been supporting my mom for the past 13 years. I pay for the rent on her two-bedroom condo. She tried to live with my sister, then me, but I couldn't handle my mom. Her culture is so different. She's always telling me how to be a wife. And I tell her, "Oh, Mom, you're not married. How can you tell me how to be a wife?"

In January of 2021, she had a hard time breathing. My brother brought her to the hospital. We found out that she was Covid-19 positive and had pneumonia. She was hospitalized for three months. She felt that without seeing family because of Covid, it wasn't worth living anymore. But she recovered and is now living with my brother.

We suffered another crisis when my youngest sister, who was a nurse for Presbyterian Memorial Hospital, killed herself. She had a chemical imbalance and insomnia, and for a whole year she'd been sleeping for only two hours and working 18 hours a day, three days a week.

My mom says depression runs in the family. When my son, David, was diagnosed with depression, I realized I needed to tell my children about the family history for medical reasons. "Why didn't you tell us?" my children asked. "You said your sister just died in her sleep." I didn't want to traumatize them then.

My dad has dementia now. He tells me about people who died many years ago. He says, "My wife, her name's Zenaida (my mom) right? And who are you again?" He had divorced his second wife, the nurse, and married a young bar girl, who turned out to be LBGTQ. She left the care of my dad to our half sister, Ashley.

Dad is not growing old gracefully. He just says whatever he feels like saying like he can smell a girl and find out whether she is a virgin or not. Perhaps at his age and what he went through to get his entire family here, he has that prerogative. But he may need to stow away again to get to heaven.

Elizabeth Jocson *is the mother of Ryan, Constance, Bo, and David. She is also the lola of Gabriella, Indigo, Gjelina, Liam, and baby Bo, ages one to nine. She lives with her husband Carlito in Nashville, Tennessee.*

Seven

NEW YORK??!!

by Winnie S. Ferrer

Start spreading the news
I'm leaving today
I want to be a part of it
New York, New York...

These are the lyrics of the classic hit which ring in my head whenever I think of New York, home for me from 1984 to 1989.

My transfer to New York was brought about by a desire for freedom from the "chains" of Philippine society's male chauvinism and traditional norms. I had just bailed out of a marriage I should not have allowed to go on for the sake of what "society would say."

I had a stable job/career so I was not wanting in this aspect. I had two children, ages nine and four, so I did my homework and had all my legal documents readied for a fresh start in a new place with a new partner. I left the Philippines with only a handful of friends and an aunt in the know.

We landed in New York and stayed for only a week since arrangements for a permanent residence was still underway. Our next stop was Maryland at the home of the brother of my very close friend, a very successful Filipino businessman who owned a travel agency and a Dunkin' Donut outlet. He loved cars and owned a Porsche! He and his wife were the perfect example of affluent Filipinos in the U.S. He asked me to stay and be his guest, which I did for a fortnight. He had three kids and this is where my own were introduced to gaming computers. I can recall climbing the snow-covered slope as their house was on a hill. Not wanting to stretch his hospitality, we transferred to a trailer owned by a friend in Virginia.

Well, New York was to my expectations, busy 24/7, but Virginia! I never expected it to be a place where we were the only living souls! Vast, beautiful, and in a quiet expanse of land, we lived in a trailer in a camp meant for summer…and it was winter! It was an experience for me as it was for my kids. One had to call a cab to go to the grocery or to church, which were miles away. I caught myself missing the tricycles and jeeps of Manila. But I was here and I had to make do and it was only temporary while my new partner was arranging his permanent job and home for all of us.

We found a small apartment in Alexandria, Virginia. It is a quaint and picturesque town and I loved it there. But this unforgettable place taught me the biggest lesson in my life—God always provides! I literally had nothing in my pocket. However, by some stroke of luck, my kids found two piggy banks filled with coins in the apartment. I called up our landlord to inquire and we were told that these had probably been left by previous tenants, so we could have them. Hurriedly, I went to the bank and exchanged the coins for paper money and on to the supermarket to buy our food!

It was not only I who had to adjust but more so my two kids. In Manila, they had all the food, clothes, and toys that they wanted. Now for the first time, I had to tell them that they could only look at the store windows as I did not have money to buy them any toys. I cannot forget the birthday of my daughter. When we had taken a cab, the driver/owner gave her a $20 bill and told her to buy herself a gift. My daughter used that money to buy all of us little gifts for Christmas.

My partner finally found a stable and decent job, so we settled in Queens Village, New York in a basement apartment. This was ideal as it was located in front of a public school, a corner away from a Catholic school to the right, and commercial establishments from the far corner at the left.

I went back to the Philippines to have my third child as the cost of a Caesarian section was too expensive considering that I was without insurance then. My partner and I decided to leave our three-month-old baby in the care of a nanny and his parents. I would pick her up after a year or so.

I returned after three months, just in time to enroll my kids in school. It was then that I realized the quality of education in the Philippines. May I point out that when they left, they had only finished five months of the grade they were in. I was so proud and happy that both of were accelerated to the next grade level. Another good point—this was a private Catholic school and it was just a few minutes' walk from our home. It meant no additional transportation costs.

As for me, it was the start of job hunting armed with all my credentials. My first attempt was at the United Nations head office where the job opening for Communication or Information Officer was right for my experience and expertise. However, I was told that in terms of my experience I was top priority but last priority in terms of nationality. In short, there were too many Filipinos working there already and other nationalities had to be given a chance. So I had to move on and scout for other opportunities.

My numerous attempts that followed were for me a grim experience. Never in my wildest dreams did I realize that my credentials became the stumbling block! "I am sorry, you will not enjoy the job! You are too educated!" was a favorite line.

I almost gave up when a Filipino friend told me to have my resume prepared by a personnel agency. I followed the advice, and the agency reduced my educational attainment from a college degree and a MBA candidacy to a second-year college student. I was given local experience with the help of my Maryland businessman/friend. So when I walked into a carpet company, I told myself that this was "now or never."

To my complete surprise, four section heads in the same company were interested in hiring me. I landed in the Export/Import Section computing taxes and tariffs on rugs and carpets that were exported and imported.

I realized then that most of the staff were high school graduates and there were only a handful with college degrees—two of the top bosses and the other Filipinos who were working in the other sections. Once I had to do the tasks assigned to my section head as she was absent. She was so shocked to find out that I had learned her job and made no secret of the fact that she was intending to hold fast onto it. I cannot forget the times I was reminded that it was lunch time and that I had to stop because the company would not pay me an additional five or ten minutes!

The greatest compliment I received was when the big boss told me that if he could only be given a free hand, he would hire Filipinos to make the whole company run. He told me, "You Filipinos are so hard working and intelligent."

I moved on to work at the Philippine Mission to the United Nations as the executive assistant of Ambassador Ingles, who was a close friend of my father. This came with a diplomatic visa, which covered all my immediate family members, and tax and other privileges. It was here where my writing, rather typing skill, was put to the test. I had an electric typewriter and then a computer. Speech after speech after speech was my daily menu! I had to be properly dressed, so I would bring my heels as I always wore my walking shoes or sneakers to walk ten blocks daily from the train station to the office at Fifth Avenue.

I faced a lot of challenges, especially with my children. I was able to walk them to school but they had to go back on their own. I would get calls from my daughter informing me that her brother refused to eat or do his homework, not realizing that my boss was in front of me and I had to maintain a straight face! The worst was when my daughter called and said that there was a lot of smoke in our apartment. I heard the wail of the fire trucks, sounds of running feet, and then silence except for the sound of the bubbles from our aquarium. I called our landlady and she told me that my kids and their cat were safe in her house. Apparently, my daughter, who loves to cook, forgot a piece of bread in the oven and it burned to a crisp, hence, the smoke! Oh my!

I was almost mugged twice: once when a tall black person tried to block me and whom I successfully dodged; another time at a subway station, three Latinos encircled me but I was able to escape by going in and out of stores until they lost sight of me. In another incident, I felt a hard slap on my back as I was walking down Fifth Avenue. A man said he mistook me for someone else! Oh yeah?! I slipped and fell down several steps going to the subway. An ambulance came almost immediately. I was checked for broken bones and bruises and informed that I could file a claim against the city as some stray newspapers scattered caused my fall. Well, I do admire New York's emergency system!

Two years down the road, I found myself with three jobs simultaneously. With the diplomatic visa, I was able to bring my third child and a nanny and this enabled my triple endeavors: my work at the Philippine Mission, assistant news editor for a Philippine-based newspaper, and a consultancy. When asked how I managed, I replied, "I just do it!"

This was New York for me. Standing out in 30-degrees-below-zero temperatures and keeping in constant motion to prevent frostbite. Believe it or not, sleeping standing up in the subway train and waking up a stop before I was to get off! On the few times I came home to Manila for a visit, I realized that I was deeply entrenched into this system that was New York. I would catch myself wondering why I was not doing anything, used as I was to having every minute count. Or speaking in

English in terms that waiters in the restaurants would not understand. Soda means soft drink!

With constant pressure from my parents, I did eventually agree to bring the children back home when my daughter was going to enter high school. I resigned from my job at the Philippine Mission, and I remember telling my boss, Ambassador Mendez, "Sir, I do hope you understand, I want to live, not merely exist!" It warms my heart every time I remember that he told me I was always welcome if I ever decided to return.

When I went back to the United States for a well-earned vacation, it was a stark difference from my years working and surviving in New York. This time I was able to watch the Broadway play "Cats," go to Studio 54 disco, watch movies, roam around; and enjoy window shopping! New York took a toll on me and my relationships, but I am stronger and wiser now…so… no regrets.

If I can make it there
I can make it anywhere
New York, New York!

In her four-decade career, **Winnie Ferrer** *has focused on the creative arts and business management. She is currently involved in public relations projects such as events, exhibits, and webinars. Active in social and political issues, joining marches and rallies, her present advocacy is the improvement and preservation of the environment. She believes that, "Life is a choice. Nothing and no one is put in your life's path by chance but rather by design in God's plan."*

Eight

FINDING FAMILY

by Margot Quema Adair

If anybody had told me that I wasn't Filipino enough, I would have been incensed, feeling insulted at such an accusation. In retrospect, I have come to admit that indeed, my identity as a Filipino was not fully formed until I first set foot on American soil. My parents were Filipino; I had a Philippine passport; I was born and had lived all my life in the Philippines until the age of 33. I looked Filipino. But in all other things, I was essentially…western. I had grown up speaking English. I considered it my first language though I spoke Tagalog and understood Ilokano.

I went to a Catholic school run by Belgian nuns, where English was the medium of instruction. The literature we read in class, the language we spoke in school, the Hollywood movies we often watched, and the music we crooned to helped shape me into having a more western outlook and to be more precise, American. On top of that, I married an American. Understandably, I often felt I was a "brown American." In fact, my first teaching job was at the American School, later called International School Manila, where I taught for nine-and-a-half years.

My journey of becoming more Filipino began in 1980 when my husband's job relocation brought us to Hawai'i. After a few years outside of the classroom, I realized that I missed the academic life—teaching and interacting with students—as well as the professional conversations I had with colleagues. And so, my first job was teaching in a federally funded bilingual program at Waipahu Intermediate to Filipino immigrant students. This led me to an epiphany.

After having taught foreign students in Manila who were children of multinational executives and embassy personnel for nine years, my new job was challenging, to say the least. My students at the American School were the children of the elite. In fact, we jokingly referred to those students as residents of the "golden ghetto" of Makati, living in a bubble. In contrast, my students in Waipahu were the children of Filipino immigrants— green-card holders who have responded to the American dream. Many of these students had put their education on hold, awaiting immigration to Hawai'i. But it is through these students that I found myself, my true identity.

My two years at Waipahu got me in touch with my Filipino roots, awakening my soul, and reconnecting with my identity. Although lacking in education, my immigrant students were rich in many other ways. They exhibited the Filipino cultural values that make anyone proud to be Filipino. They were filial, respectful of elders. Their parents had a strong work ethic, in which Filipinos pride themselves. Many of them worked two jobs, sometimes three, making it difficult to have face-to-face conferences but they wrote me notes, sharing their concerns for their children. I saw the unconditional love they had for their children, the dreams and aspirations they were carving out for them, and their conviction that hard work would emancipate them from poverty. After all, wasn't this what America was all about?

When I looked at my students as they struggled to understand the lesson, I felt overwhelmed by the challenges of bilingual teaching. I am reminded of that line in Emma Lazarus' poem, "Give me your tired, your poor, your huddled masses yearning to breathe free . . ." These kids and their families had fled the homeland, escaping the tyranny of poverty, political

Real and extended family (top to bottom): FAUW and mahjong group Bing Pepi, Mylene, Margot, Nanette; sons Dicky and Alex; best friends Choleng (left) and Virgie (in green) with sisters Menchu and Marilen.

instability, and the bleakness of a future of dreams deferred. Here they were sitting in the classroom, hopeful and eager leaners while their parents juggled several jobs to make their dreams come true. I realized that I had taken the real meaning of family—making sacrifices and loving each other—for granted.

My Filipino immigrant students were the catalyst for my search for family in my adopted home. Because of them, I realized I missed my large extended family—my parents, my siblings and their children, and my numerous aunts, uncles, and cousins. I had been "Tita" to so many of my nieces and nephews and missed hearing that. I missed the sound of my voice calling out to my older sister, "Manang." I pined for those Sunday family lunches, the celebrations of birthdays, family weddings, and Christmases. I realized that there was much truth to the adage that one only realizes what is valuable when she has lost it. Family is what I lost, that sense of belonging, of being part of a bigger whole, a safe haven when things go awry, a warm heart and soft shoulder with which to share the ups and downs of life.

I regretted how I felt constricted by family obligations and expectations in the past, avoiding family gatherings or feeling suffocated by family expectations. Sometimes, I escaped family gatherings because I felt that family members invaded my sense of privacy, asking too many nosy questions about my personal life. But now, somehow, I missed being part of family.

When I became a parent, my 68-year-old mother really gave me an even deeper appreciation of family when she helped take care of my children. Mommy came to help me because I would be going back to teaching. She was making the ultimate sacrifice, leaving behind the comforts of home, her social circle of friends, and her daily mahjong games. She came because that's what family is all about, making sacrifices for love of family.

As my boys grew up, passing on Filipino values became essential. Family always came first. Helping and watching out for each other became my mantra to my two sons. Respect for elders was non-negotiable. My two boys quickly learned that our friends were to be called "Tita" or "Tito," no first-name calling as was the norm here in America.

When my mother left to go back home, I felt her absence intensely. How does one recapture the sense of family, as I knew it, here in America where the nuclear family is the norm? I found this, most notably, at FAUW (Filipino Association of University Women), meetings where connections became stronger as we discovered shared experiences of growing up, of the values with which our parents had raised us including demanding family obligations and discipline. My mahjong group became another lifeline. When I am with them, we become one family, exchanging stories about our children and grandkids, our family traditions, our college dating days, our favorite actors and actresses in Chinese and Korean dramas. At the end of our mahjong sessions, there is the ritual of preparing our baon (take-home foods), replicating every Filipino get-together's wrapping up of food for our loved ones left at home. My new extended family has become my strength especially through my deepest encounter of loss. They ushered me through my husband's illness and eventual passing. When I got seriously ill, this family jumped in to care for my needs.

Athough my fate has allowed me to metamorphose into my American self—speaking, dressing, often thinking like an American—this journey has only heightened my acknowledgment that, if someone probes into my soul, one can clearly perceive its native color and temperament: the emphasis on filial piety and respect, a passion for sacrifice and hard work, the deep shade of love and loyalty. These are what family has taught me. This is what makes me celebrate my Filipino legacy.

 **Margot Adair** started her teaching career at the International School of Manila. Upon relocating to Honolulu, she first taught at the Hawai'i Department of Education as a bilingual and ESL teacher. Later, she taught at Maryknoll School until her retirement after 30 years.

Nine

RECOVERING MEMORY

by Maya

Fate was preparing me for exile.

At the latter part of my college years, in the late sixties, my heart and mind in turmoil, I welcomed everything optional. Latin, French, modern ballet, art club, theatre…"the best in the West!" Was I caught in the esoteric forces behind the world-youth unrest? Or was it the new experiences outside our all-girl kolehiyo (college)? New exchanges with male editors from different universities, or those isms from far away? Dark nihilism, irreverent existentialism…who knows? My personal colonization had reached its apogee with competent Belgian sisters, lyrical Catholicism in my identity. But I felt growing in me a new rush, not for gold but for truth, historical truth.

After graduation, granted a scholarship for an MS in Sociology and economics, I left for Manila. This migration to the capital would be the first stop on a long journey towards life in exile. My parents insisted on joining me, primarily to thank the Asian Social Institute (ASI) for my scholarship. Unnecessary, said the West in me. But my parents of "Old Philippines" believed in active gratitude; heaven's wrath—Gaba!—strikes the ingrate. To my surprise, this was quite appreciated.

I was happy in ASI, my family in Manila, with Fr. Senden at its head, a Rock-of-Gibraltar for some, for me a whole universe. My inexperience was counseled by working adults; they were already contributing to society. The Institute was action-oriented, so it was less boring than studying virtual reality. Knowledge would be constantly put to test. The universal constant being un-constant, being change, everything human is perishable in time and space.

The first years in Manila would reveal, in studies and field exposure, situations of grave injustice in rural and urban areas. We were all students of sociology and economics, intertwined sciences, though in real life, economics tends to lord it over sociology. Governments get elected on promises of bringing food closer to the poor man's mouth. Yup, as close as the curse of Tantalus! Though here, people are innocent.

Graduate studies were humbling. My shoulders heavy with ignorance, I went from question to question, as a long journey in chaos. I'd later discover that a pensive question on the background of social reality can already hold the seed of an answer. But, but...

I was molting. My vision began to mutate. We had a project on estero (canal) dwellers in Pasay. On a background of filth and grime, like sunlight in chronic dusk, a luminous nobility. There he stood, well tatooed, in our free clinic, his sick baby lovingly in his arms, its limp hand on his long black hair, on his naked chest trustingly. Or a lovely little boy, earnestly explaining his absence at nursery school, who ran errands for his mom, gathering firewood in a woodless slum. Or those we met in town, God-fearing persons, lay or religious, with lucid spirituality, the luminous few who dared act on conviction, dared to stand on the side of the poorest, armed with faith, a strong heart for compatriots. The struggle would be long.

Remember the racist legend about God wanting to bake a perfect human? The first undercooked, the second burnt, the third nicely brown? Tried this on my nursery class. Finally, God was pleased with ...? "Pilipino!" they all cried out. So, who's the most perfect, the most pogi (handsome)? In one voice: "Amerikano! GI Joe!" their little eyes beaming. Served me right!

But there were sacred moments, working together, memorizing laws, the Land Reform Code, restudying Philippine history, evoking the first days of Christianity when men's devotion to God was pure and free. They were beautiful, in chiaroscuro, the chords playing, our singing, writing poetry, in dialogue with the youth of the land, feeling one in poverty, fighting misery and despair.

Poverty, my sociological, metaphysical conclusion. NOT extreme deprivation which destroys, dehumanizes. I want that poverty with nothing yet everything, a poverty that gains by sharing. One Philippine chieftain said it: a man's wealth can only be measured by his capacity to share.

I did not want to leave the Philippines, the motherland that shaped my soul, gave me depth, gave me family, gave me all! The idea of going abroad, in normal times, and temporarily, could thrill the monkey in me, but this timing was wrong. So many tasks undone, budding relationships to enlighten and develop, many more dreams to fulfill at home. Exile was a death sentence!

But, alas, alas! A dark, despotic monster lurked on the horizon. It had limited intelligence. It couldn't discern differences, took each critique as aggression, Christian or communist, armed or un-armed, whether the count was in dollars or weight in power. I was advised to get out. Murky agents were making the round of schools, waiting for instructions to eliminate. My family agreed. I had to go. It was my last chance, before the great disaster.

I stayed in Cebu, the moment of a last goodbye, made a bonfire of my writings. Paternal Lolo, my first hero who refused to serve the Spaniards, had passed away and Lola, in her late 90s, wasn't quite with us anymore. But I took the four-hour bus ride to see her at the farm, for a last amin. Did she recognize me? Anyway, she still gave her typical simhut kiss, went on and on about my life abroad, as if I had already left. Missed out on chronology, but her deep lucidity was intact.

Despite the pain of separation, the anxiety before a dark unknown, I felt strengthened by family affection. Papa's set rules became more precious than ever. At table, he was protecting not only digestion but our nerves. I'd realize this later, strong nerves are a great advantage in neurotic West, a great armor.

Nothing's perfect in humanity, but I felt consoled with one thought: despite errors in life, my family could stand on the side of justice. Even maternal Lolo who'd sit quietly, watching our huddle with friends, in serious reflection. One day he finally intervened, "Promise me, that when things get really rough, you will never give up. Beware of those in power..." Those words, and a special dish he cooked for me, were his last farewell.

I just had enough time to say goodbye to friends in Manila. They came to the airport, with addresses and recommendations for Italy, Spain, England. I boarded the plane, my dear cousin next to me, clasping those envelopes, my aching heart calling on the monkey in me, for a smile. Flying off to another world was, after all, an adventure!

England was my first real stop. Along with personal effects, I smuggled homegrown confusion. With the lingering dark clouds of a colonial past, I slipped packs of colorful sunsets and the sweet perfume of humble blooms. There were spirit-pockets of trees and bird songs, little scents of the sacred, like butterfly hues on weeds. The chest was full of promises. I didn't come as conquistador, I'd be respectful of European natives, I'd humbly learn.

But, first things first...my mission to meet third-world activists or sympathizers. They came in all shades of mental and physical colors, with varying degrees of sincerity and sympathy. I'd inform about the current Philippine situation, our home struggle with victims of injustice. But I wasn't ready for the noise, the great excitement midst activists (back home, we were whispering in public places), not to mention the chismis (and I thought noise and chismis were a Philippine invention)! The air of absolute freedom was worrying.

Yet, in all that, my good memory of African women, my first friends in the island, who gave warmth to cold London, our exchanges in community, family, their ever-present children. We could relate with common values, in moments of worry and laughter.

I had to re-think the sense of this exile, of home expectations, my capacity to continue the struggle, the passion. By then, my cousin's departure for the U.S. had left me alone, with limited energy. How to handle a growing suspicion of all political?

Instead of lessons in frenzied manipulation, I opted for quiet, serious observation, reflection, seeking out the truth of peoples, exploring new pathways.

I said I'd learn from the natives, didn't I? So, I left the urban chaos and sought refuge in the lovely English countryside, enrolled in a general nursing school where majority of students were high school dropouts. The only Filipina and older, rumored to have "more degrees than a thermometer," I had a respectful rapport with classmates. Despite colonial-minded teachers, we had Mr. H, a caring principal-tutor.

One day, in the media, the tragedy. Martial Law was declared back home. Mr. H then called me to his office to express condolences. I can still see him behind the desk, a box of tissues on one hand, when the tears flowed. He knew what I was going through, he said, the new environment, the fact that I didn't "suffer fools gladly." And he knew, Martial Law hurt.

Amnesty International showed me its long list of political prisoners. They'd visit and assist those who were not into armed struggle.

By then, the pull of destiny was taking me away from nursing. After working months in a psychiatric hospital, I finally gave up. Home Office warned me. They didn't like foreigners who moved around freely. Hmmm, their idea of democracy, I imagine.

Psychiatric nursing was most interesting but trying. My problem? A personal issue with truth and reality. It really hurts when you're constantly battered with un-truth. For me, it was obvious, each mental patient was a tomb of suffering, buried with drugs. Very few went home. I'd see lovers kiss and cuddle, seemingly happy, but for their zombie gait. Our own lovable, taciturn Mr. Smith, his vest stuffed with old newspaper, with his habit of lying on his tummy on the cold earth to chat with earthworms. One day, watching TV, he talked to me and declared he was a prince! Ah! Reminded me of a younger "royalty" in another ward who claimed to be a Russian princess. She spoke with a foreign accent but was in fact very English. After disappearing from home, she ended up with us. Her family came, pleaded, but she had gone too far in delusion. Mr. Jones was quiet, at breakfast table, he'd sway, his shoulders in seesaw, to the left, to right "to insure earth's balance" said he. "Thank you!" I'd say. Each patient, a story presumed untrue, still deserves true affection and respect.

I missed university life and applied for a double diploma in political science and linguistics, majoring French. My interviewer did not understand the American unit system, but claimed to perceive my positive, energetic nature. On this was I admitted, on condition that I spend all summer in France before school opening.

Yet, those months in Paris opened other facets of European life, its intriguing contradictions and the pull of artistic creation. This Maya bird found its companion and was ready to build a nest this part of the West. England was but a stop-over on the way to France the beauty, my real destiny.

In fact, elegant Paris would be my harshest, abroad. In the English countryside, I felt protected by a migrant population within hospital walls. France, the land of high science and laws, was another story. I was exposed to wind and fire! With little French, how could I engage in intelligent dialogue? I had to learn the local tongue quickly, to build an armor, to fight my way through another migrant battlefield.

Mama's mantra was Divine Providence. In migration, I add Courage, Lucidity, Invention. She once said, when you're invited to dine at foreign tables, it's safest to simply follow the host or hostess (though I was told of a dinner hosted by a ministry, where a diplomat's wife started smoking after the main dish, obliging the host to cover the outrage by smoking himself). On a wider perspective, it's equivalent to looking for the best model, whether linguistic or behavioral.

Respect the native, speak his language properly, I said. My girl-school education came handy in England, though I had to shake off my well-practiced American. So, how to speak like a Parisian native? I watched the French speak on TV and in person, watched their facial anatomy to figure out which muscles to use. Just the time to know the fowl's anatomy, in my first try at cooking. I finally learned to dismember chicken and speak the rooster's tongue at the same time (Gallic rooster, French symbol)!

The power of the tongue. Over here, majority of Filipinas are employed as domestic workers; they became my new advocacy. Holding French lessons for some, was education for me. Now and then, they'd moan, "How to retaliate when a French partner, with drinking friends, blabber racist or snide remarks about us?!" I'd start with reminders. Many feel degraded as "atsay" or "tsimay (maids)." Those words had to go, for good! With dignity must we break the demon of inferiority, reflected in social mirrors. I had to distribute "arms" for my students: relevant vocabulary and some French history, focusing on events that racists don't want to know.

Working in private homes, especially as "live-in" can favor a new form of colonization. Filipinas in awe of their rich amo (master) may tend to absorb their thinking.

A Filipina is a complex institution. We're a house with many doors, barriers, and traps. When we're asked questions, we tend to re-ask, in private: "What do you want me to say? Do I have to please you? How? What are your intentions? Will you hurt me? How do I protect myself?" guarding truth only for friends. Impossible to answer a purely yes or no question. Instinctively we know, it doesn't exist.

Maya (second from right) with artists who are domestic workers at a painting exhibit in the Paris Philippine fiesta.

Europe is many Europes: intelligent, compassionate Europe, or racist, xenophobic and ignorant Europe. My centenarian mom tends to say: "America is not a place to bring up children." Europe too? Well, there's really only one place to bring up a child: in the family or tribe.

In 1908, Polish grand-uncle, Kazimierz Jezewski, created the Society of Orphan Nests that took orphans out of the orphanage and into farm families. Poland, rich in history and culture, shares our values of extended family, a long tradition of heroism, spirituality, generosity. Our children take such pride in being half-Pinoy, half-Polish.

Someone asked what Philippine legacy I'd leave them. Besides my history, my being, my values? Here's one: respect for food.

Back home, we didn't sit for breakfast uncombed, with unwashed faces. Not to please the company or practice good manners. It was in respect of food, each meal being sacred, a moment of grace and gratitude. Papa never allowed rowdy behavior, violent arguments, or unpleasant stories while eating. He forbade money or anything unclean on the dining table. Always and foremost, respect for food. I still cringe at rice-throwing after weddings, at stepping on rice grains!

Another element to consider while abroad is friendliness. Filipinas are a charming people. But, quite often, problems arise when we don't know limits in friendly behavior. We tend to adopt *nice* people as family, even employers. Yet, what really counts at work is not being nice but professional, demanding respect.

Smile! Smile is a form of (Philippine) defense. And yet, like all things in life, it's multi-edged. It can be taken as a sign of stupidity (for a cold Frenchman, an easy smiler's *primaire*, simple-minded). It can warm a lonely heart, it can also be taken as an invitation. My experience says, better learn to un-smile in public places, with unfamiliar persons. Bear a look of confidence that keeps beasts at bay. Build a bubble of family and friends; outside, it's safer to distrust, to bar entry into your life, your personal, your intimate. Be a good listener, help when you can, open to true friendship but, take time for a good look, a good think. Keep the front door locked. This is not our home-village anymore; this is abroad.

I often say that I brought up my children the Philippine way. They said they'd do the same. But can they, being French too? In their early years, I'd send them out of the country on summer or winter holidays to family in Cebu, to close cousins in the U.S., to good friends in London, Cologne, to give perspective, my wish that each positive experience inhabit their subconscious. They once thanked me for "teaching the art of happiness!" Did I? When?

France the highly permissive, obsessed with liberté, often forgetting the rest of the package (fraternité, egalité), holds a grudge against the sacred; fun and seduction tend to replace love and respect for the other. So, parenting here is "wading in sauerkraut," laborious! At eight, my son tearfully: "Mama, why did you teach us to be honest? It is sooo difficult!"

It has taken years of solitude in exile, from alien to citizen, reflecting on our history, our pain, confusion, humiliation, inspired by Philippine courage and resilience, to grow into another form of humanity. Such a long way to knowing the heart and soul of past tormentors, looking back to those centuries of falsehood. The myth of whiteman's superiority, our inferiority, baloney!

With deep compassion, shall we pray: "Forgive them Lord, for they didn't know?" Forgiveness. Immense but immense! To ask forgiveness demands courage, lucidity. To forgive demands wisdom.

Ex-colonizers are dead and buried, but their mentality survives arrogantly, in their descendants and, sadly, in us. Their guilt in denial, preference for historical amnesia; we integrate the colonial maze that tries to tolerate us. We're always tempted to say yes to a globalized logic of material progress and frenzied consumerism, promising happiness and contentment.

Colonization a continuing reality, decolonization a must. Ex-victims can't build a life on hatred and resentment. But colonization is addictive, colonizers can't let go! The struggle is now on our side, to de-victimize, to exorcise the demons they brought in and left behind. Holding truth is a gift to manage with utmost lucidity.

I now realize that leaving home was for reasons beyond pesky politics. Each Filipina who believes in her capacity to change can also reconnect with sacred tribal values. For a strong Philippine identity, we need to recapture and live their original meaning and practice, to complete the alchemy, the faith that turns a dark colonial past into a luminous future.

I know, good things are happening back home, despite odds, with the righteous who chose to stay. Already, many recognize the innate intelligence of our peasants, in their once bothersome "resistance to change," their instinct, to protect environment. For (western) science can serve business interests and damn farmers to dependence on chemicals, slowly but surely killing the land and its people. In response, new eco-movements sprout here and there in the Philippines, in search of old reliables, indigenous plants and trees that know their pests. In the memory of an illness may lie the secret of its cure.

I'm writing this in perspective from France, a mothership of colonization. The question of identity that never bothered me in the Philippines is bothering now. At home, I felt so good under my skin, in my family and tribe, in a present that shouldn't have changed. Digging into my past, our past, I remember things I took for granted. I remember them now.

Translations:

Amin	*blessing*
Amo	*master*
Chismis	*gossip*
Gaba!	*heaven's wrath*
Pwera usog	*exclamation to ward off evil*
Simhut	*inhaling kiss*

A Cebuana, born the year of the monkey, **Maya** *was part of a peaceful Christian movement before leaving the Philippines. But Martial Law, its dictatorship in advanced paranoia, couldn't distinguish one cause from another. Oriented towards sociology back home, she'd continue in France. She joined Babaylan association (at that time linked with a European network and French anti-slavery groups), addressing issues of violence and unfair labor practice. She then discovered that our women who feel degraded by their new status as domestic workers are actually a gifted lot. Babaylan would find ways to expose their literary, musical, and artistic talents.*

Wife to a Polish writer, mother of two graphic artists, grandmother to three gems (pwera usog!), she's now a retired elderly. As such, she hopes to realize her dream of a happy poverty, conducive to creation and sharing. Her books of poetry, illustrated with her paintings and sketches, were published in Poland and France.

Ten

EAST AND WEST: THE TWAIN DO MEET

by Gina M. Ordonez

It's raining outside, drops on my window pane and grey clouds hovering over the Makati sky, perfect for looking back at an adult life half-spent in the U.S and the other half in Manila. I am now in my seventies and have lived through bitter-sweet memories from both countries. Living in another country in the seventies and early eighties was not called the "diaspora," it was called the "American dream."

Not only did America teach me the ropes of living on my own, but it also gave me the privilege of two graduate degrees on some form of scholarship.

My job history spanned from the East Coast of the United States to the Pacific Islands of Hawai'i. When I was young, just out of college, I dreamed of living in New York, and made that dream come true. I took on an airline job and, after two years, earned a free flight to New York where the usual thing for a tourist visa holder was to convert it into a legal stay by the fastest way, a job in the United Nations. There I was exposed to the global development issues which were the bread and butter of the U.N. Thrown into this international cultural work group, I mixed with them, but on days off, preferred the more socially comfortable company of my own Filipino friends.

Not that it mattered much, since it was the thrill of Broadway plays and museums at the Big Apple on weekends that took me to the stars. Also, I could gaze nightly upon the brightly lit skyline of New York City from my West New York condo where I roomed with two other Filipinas, one a cousin, and both from Manila's College of the Holy Spirit.

But it wasn't good enough; I needed to move on. And move on I did, to Northern California to pick up my first graduate degree. I roomed with an Iranian girl. Since there were few Filipinos on campus, I would travel to San Francisco from time to time to meet up with my own kind. At least we could speak about the latest events in the Philippines, swap stories about prominent and school-connected families whom we either knew personally or knew of, and we could sense the meaning of each other's body language; non-verbal signals were sufficient to convey discomfort or disapproval around others.

I moved back to the Philippines to repay my scholarship dues and worked for a government training institute. But after two years, I returned to the U.S. This time my destination was Washington D.C., where my parents and a brother lived. There the Filipino community was much larger since it was home to the World Bank, the International Monetary Fund (IMF), and lots of embassies so that Filipinos could take their pick of a job without losing their legal status as residents.

Within the walls of my George Washington University office, the streets of Penn Avenue and Georgetown, or the homes and malls in Arlington or Alexandria, I never felt any disparity between brown versus white, nor the discomfort of being what some call a "second-class citizen" in a foreign land. Perhaps it was because I had been brought up with English as my first language, and so it was second nature to me to speak it naturally and fluently. Or perhaps I was blessed with a self-confidence in thinking that I was as good as anyone else.

Unfortunately, I could never whip up Filipino dishes that would bring in bunches of Filipino friends to gather at the whiff of any occasion, nor got good enough at any of the mahjong

97

games played on weekends by those working at the World Bank or the embassies. So I just became a tag-along in these Filipino gatherings. It was all part of the adventure of "living abroad."

However, I was driven away by the cold winters of the East. Again, I returned to the Philippines, this time joining the ranks of the then-reputed top Asian graduate school of business. While the professorial work was intellectually stimulating with students from India all the way to Indonesia, yet another cross-cultural experience, I began to feel uneasy with the increasingly pervasive culture of amorality fed by corruption and cronyism amidst the pervading fear of the Marcos dictatorship, which by then was running about seven years.

I began to see America as the place where my social ways would be more acceptable, and my expectations of institutional rules met. There I could drive without traffic jams, line up to catch a bus or subway that arrived and left on time, walk blocks at a time through condos and parks in non-polluted air, expect people to come on time, say what they thought, and do their best at work.

I decided to leave the country again. Having been offered a scholarship at the University of Hawai'i, I was glad to pack my bags and take off for the State of Liquid Sunshine. My friends there were a combination of the mostly academic Filipino community and colleagues at work. With regular beach picnics, socio-civic group gatherings, and weekend stays with a typical dual-culture local family, the husband a white haole and his wife a child of Ilocano parents who had migrated to Hawai'i, I breezed through my study program. I brushed off ideas that "island fever" might get to me if I stayed too long.

The East-West Center had such a blend of nationalities, all merging and sometimes marrying each other; mixed racial couples were a common sight. After getting my degree, however, I decided to travel back to California where my family had moved. They lived on Redondo Beach, Los Angeles, which was a great attraction to me since I loved walking the shoreline. Back came the Filipino family tradition of going together to Sunday Mass and lunch. Racial differences were not of much consequence at my job at Epson America. I felt on par with those of other cultures and colors but this was short-lived since the company was forced to downsize.

The Ordonez siblings with President Cory Aquino. (l to r) Ernie and wife Sylvia, President Aquino, Gina, and Victor.

Hawai'i beckoned to me again with its calm and relaxed lifestyle. I re-started a new life there and concluded that I had found my paradise with its swaying palm trees, gentle tropical climate, and the spirit of ohana or family, where I had hoped to settle down for a long time. If ever I could choose a permanent residence to live in, this would be the ideal place.

But life had other plans for me. The miracle that was EDSA ONE struck, becoming the pride of the Filipino people, a peaceful yet successful resistance to the dictatorship after the martyrdom of Benigno Aquino, Jr. By this time, I had read and heard enough of the injustices in Philippine society perpetrated by a government that ruled with an iron hand on the common people. I was angry but could do nothing. But the stories were burnt into my heart and mind and would affect my decision to return again to my homeland.

I announced to whoever was interested that I had to go back to help the nation get back on its feet, and rise to become a newly industrialized country, or NIC. I had dreams that poor families would be able to join the ranks of the middle class, with fair and equitable opportunities to get out of the poverty cycle.

Filled with hope and the promise of a better future for my people, and led by the yellow-bannered President Corazon Aquino, I joined development agencies and non-government organizations, NGOs. The exhilarating politics of it, the meaningfulness of a job that was more like a calling, the hobnobbing with people in key positions were a good start.

Here I was back in Manila, supposedly a big fish in a small pond; where in the U.S., I was just a small cog in a big wheel. Here I could be part of making a significant difference in people's lives; there, I was just one of a crowd of driven professionals. Here I was as much a conference attendee as a party girl; there it was just an 8:00 to 5:00 job occupying my time, then home to housework and simple living.

I re-discovered the values of family, connections and networking, hospitality and generosity, sensitivity to others, the importance of body language, group preferences rather than individual choices.

As a family member, I was invited to sumptuous foodie reunions of both my mother's and father's clans, sometimes 50 or more gathered, while in the U.S. only a handful of friends could meet socially every so often for a comparatively simple meal. Manila meant having a lifestyle that included relatively inexpensive house help and driver service that made it possible for me to concentrate on my work demands as well as my social life without worrying about the everyday details of living—cooking, cleaning, washing and ironing clothes, cleaning the car, etc. It was the opposite of the daily drudgery in the U.S. of having to do everything for one's self at home.

Here family meant everything, a support system guaranteed to help other members who grew old or had less resources. Catholic rituals were alive, with churches packed on Sundays, and colorful processions for fiestas. Music and dance were a prominent activity, with sing-along karaoke bars beckoning one and all to sing their hearts out till the wee hours of the morning.

My long years in the U.S. had shaped me into a balikbayan (returnee to home country) whose nationalistic heart loves the Philippines, but whose standards do not jibe with the "yes" that actually meant "no" or "maybe." I was surprised at the sensitivity felt by people who take personally any frank but contrary words with no intent to harm. Doctor and government office appointment times were casually ignored so that ordinary citizens had to wait for hours for service. Social connections still dominated the ability to get and move up in a job. Class consciousness is imbedded in the haves versus the have-nots, and self-entitlement drove the former to treat the latter as inferior.

Americans visiting the country generally love Filipinos and our culture and bring home with them experiences that put reality to the tourism tag, "It's more fun in the Philippines." They smile back at the smiling faces of the poor children. They are welcomed as family or friend and enter the luxury homes of the upper class if they have the right connections. They forget about the inconveniences of unclean toilets, delayed planes, rough roads, "facilitation fees" for speedier service, and all that goes along with the package of being a "developing country."

But I strained at the bit, insisting on more efficiency, more punctuality, more action than talk, in the things we did, in the projects we engaged in, in the staff we relied on. But after all, this was not America.

Why the diaspora? The majority of Filipinos leave their native land for a better economic future. Primary in their hearts is their family's need for food, health, and education, to help relatives mired in poverty. They work in the US and other lands to bring home the bread from more advanced economies.

As with the Chinese, Koreans, and Japanese, Filipinos tend to stick to their own, but we do not form a small town in a foreign country. There is no extensive neighborhood known as a Filipino town (although there are blocks with predominantly Filipino residents) in the way Chinatown or Korean town exist. Having come from a country whose Malay race was mixed in with Chinese traders and entrepreneurs, Spanish colonial masters for 300 years, then American do-gooders for another 50, Filipinos meld more easily into other cultures.

But in the end, seeing that fateful attack on Capitol Hill in Washington, D.C. by generally white supremacists on January 6, 2021, it seems, after all, that America is not really a country of equals which welcomes, as inscripted on New York City's Statue of Liberty, "the tired, the poor, the huddled masses yearning to be free." Not now anyway.

Now I see that defects in Philippine society are also present in western society. Corruption exists at all levels even if it is much more palpable in the Philippines where Filipinos are more aware of how people accumulated their wealth. Vested interests flourish in both countries. Power and greed will always be a strong motivator for people, whether black, brown, yellow, or white. American institutions are stronger, more impersonal, with a history of laws and standards that keep the general public in check with rules. In the Philippines, it is more a free-for-all, with a more personalized approach to getting things done since institution-building remains at an early stage.

The universal human tendency to mix with your own kind, to deal with issues of Me vs. You, or We vs. Them, can be overcome only if mutual respect and acceptance are nurtured. With globalization, comparisons and contrasts among diverse cultures are easier seen. Yet we all are the same under the different colors of our skin.

I look out my window to the now blue skies and ponder over the 50 adult years I have lived. I have taken the best of both worlds; on one hand; the familiar closeness and support of family and friends, and on the other, the desire to achieve on my own merits. Compromises have had to be made. Dissatisfaction and frustration, as well as an urge to get things and people changed for the better good, remain.

But my Filipino psyche, my Filipino self, looks to God and trusts Him for the answers, and to his Mother Mary for succor. I rest in the knowledge that the God Who is for all, the God of both East and West unites us all in Him.

*For more than 30 years, **Gina M. Ordonez** has been consulting, researching, and writing on management, planning, and education. She was a professor at the Asian Institute of Management in Makati and De La Salle University/Taft, Manila. An East-West Center grantee, she earned her MBA at the University of Hawai'i while working as assistant director at the UH's College of Business-Management Programs Center for overseas students. She established a consultancy firm, Quantum Learning Institute. Now retired, Gina enjoys her two grandsons, Jason and Joey, while still carrying the torch of hope for the country's socio-economic future through advocacy and assistance to poor communities.*

Eleven

POEMS BY AN IMMIGRANT WOMAN

by Maria Llanes Quema

To Thee, I Pledge

Back and forth, I go over the chapters of my life,
Though memories belong to the distant past.
My native land, friends, and relatives
are core and part of my life.
The truth is the past that will always be present,
And the future a part!

I can't dismiss the heritage from my Filipino father.
He was a lawyer, a judge, a great lawmaker.
Nor can I discard the rich Spanish culture of my mother.
To forget all is to lose my identity.
'Tis no easy matter!

I'm grateful for an education quite far from the ordinary,
An amalgamate of three cultures,
Distinct but in essence, not far apart.
After a serious soul searching, I want to be an American.
Home is where your heart is. America is my home!
How proud I'd be to belong to this "sweet land of liberty!"
To love and serve her with my undivided loyalty!

The late **Maria Llanes Quema** wrote these poems after deciding to live in America with her children. Found by her daughter Margot Quema Adair, the poems reflect the immigrants' desire for a new life in a new land while longing for the sweet sounds and sights of home.

104

Hermosos Recuerdos*

Back and forth, I stroll along my private memory lane,
A favorite pastime that does not cause me a dime,
My wayward thoughts dwelling on friends, food, and wine,
And family members long gone and three sisters getting along fine.

With my cronies, I'd like to play mahjong,
Once more to hear the sounds of 'chow', 'kang' and 'pong!'
Patiently, I'll listen to their chatter and repeated tales of affliction,
For whom I'd care to hear with sympathy and warm affection.

I think of atis, chico, lanzones, and mango,
Chicharron, ludong, and gakka from Aparri shared by
Nacing Pablo
I like nateng, and dried fish with that heavenly smell.
Alas! To others it's a very far cry from Coco Chanel!

I remember a long dining table in Casa Llanes.
My father and brother arguing, 'cause that's what lawyers do,
My mother quietly leaving to play her own concerto,
My brother, Eming, not far behind.

Eming played jazz and classical together, a feat of wizardry!
He played on heartstrings and carried you on magical planes.
When he played "Campanella" everything was history!
Would that I could recapture those wondrous strains!

*Beautiful Memories

WHO WE ARE

Twelve

AN AMERICAN WOMAN IN A FILIPINA BODY

by Rene Brock

I am a Filipino girl, now a grown woman, who was raised in the United States.

A question that I pondered throughout my life: "Who am I? Am I an American or a Filipino?" Let me begin by telling you my story...

I was born in the Philippines in 1967. At 13 days old, I was adopted by an American couple. My father was a naval officer and my mother was a naval nurse. My parents dreamed of having children, but my mother was unable to carry a child, so they decided to adopt and begin their own family. They both prayed for a baby to hold and raise as their own. This would surely be a blessing from God.

My time in the Philippines was short; I do not have any memory of it because I was only there for the first three years of my life. The only thing that I have are old videos taken in the islands, where my parents would chase me around the yard. They showed so much happiness since their wish for a child came true.

Approximately three years later, I was brought to America. I was raised by and with Americans and went to the United States Court to receive my official citizenship. I ate American cuisine, went to school and church, and was raised with family values like any other child. Sports were a big part of the American culture, as well as holidays and recreational activities.

As I grew older, I remember how I always wanted to fit in. I had the Asian look in the middle of a community of white Americans. However, my parents adopted another baby girl from the Philippines when my father was based in Subic Bay. She was ten months younger. She was a person I could always identify with since she was also Filipina, although I must say, she had much bigger eyes. Some would say we were twins because of our age, but I always thought we looked quite different. My sister Laurie would be told that she was from the brown people. She was able to handle what I felt was criticism with more stride, while I was never that strong and confident.

As a young girl, I went to a rural elementary school. I will never forget going into my classroom and sitting in the first row by the wall. The boy behind me kept saying, "Where's your boat? Go back to Cambodia!" I just ignored him and did not say anything. Unfortunately, I was not armed with a quick rebuttal to validate who I was, one of God's children. I also remember the slang term of "chink" which meant that one was Chinese with chinky eyes. I felt like crawling into a hole or running to my papa to protect me. My appearance was always questioned and I began to grow insecure. I felt out of place, wondering if there were any other Asians in the community. When I finally was acquainted with another Asian girl, I was not sure I wanted to associate with her, since we might have been needlessly ridiculed and chastised even more in the rigid, close-minded school climate.

Women's magazines and newspaper ads selling beauty products in America demonstrated the profile of what a "pretty American girl" should look like. The desired look was blonde hair and blue eyes. This was emulated by the "Barbie" doll that so many young girls associated with. Barbie is a tall, long blonde-haired model with blue eyes and a flawless figure. The company also created "Ken" a male doll who could be Barbie's boyfriend. Ken was also portrayed as an American boy, with a fancy Corvette and a nice home with a pool in the backyard.

This was the "American Dream." I did not see myself fitting into this part of the typical, beautiful, "American" image. In fact, I thought the most outstanding quality I had was my hooded eye. Some people would tell me that they could not see my eyes when I smiled. I felt so uneasy and insecure, I preferred to be the "quiet one" in a crowd. I thought of ways to fix my eye.

Surgery, make-up, or mascara might be a solution, but to no avail; it was something that I had to live with. My parents always told me I had a "different look," a beautiful look because it was exotic. Wow! Would I have felt special if I had been seen this way? Most girls in the Philippines must be exotic and beautiful. What would it be like if I were to live there? I knew this would never happen. I was living in the United States. I just wanted to be like all the other American girls. I was used to the American way of life. I did not have any exposure to the Filipino community, nor to its culture. I felt lost in my own skin. I was an American girl in a Filipina body.

Although my parents spoke of my "unique and special look," they never spoke of the Philippines. I thought that they did not want me to know too much about my native land. After all, I was now living in America, and they did not want me to inquire about my birth parents.

My American family consisted of my mom, my dad, my sister, and brother. We were a typical American family. Family was important; I was raised by both an Italian family on my mother's side and a German family on my father's side. Both sides of my family loved me as if I were their own; adoption was rarely brought up in conversation.

As time went on, I began to ask about the Philippines. My mom would then share some stories, such as the tornadoes, the cuisine, Alice our housekeeper, and our nanny Wilma. Wilma held a special place in our family. She was with my parents every day and helped to raise my sister and me. Years after we left the islands, Wilma also left for the United States when she married an American man who was in the military. Wilma always kept in touch with my parents, as they were very fond of her. She was my only connection to the Philippines; she was the one who had the look of a Filipino, who spoke the language, as well as introduced our taste buds to Filipino food. I loved her dishes, the rice, and her warm heart. I always thought of her as my own relative. She took care of me as if I were her own child.

In 1972, Wilma traveled to Maine with my family so my parents could adopt my brother. She spent several weeks with us, and I loved her presence. I could see a reflection of myself, my nationality, and my homeland. It was not often that this happened to me. Over the years, we went our separate ways. Wilma and the family always exchanged Christmas cards and frequent phone calls, but our visits were rare.

In 1990, I married an American of Hungarian and German descent. He had light hair and green eyes. Even when I was brought to his home for the first time, his folks questioned my look—was I Chinese or Japanese? I had always resented this because I just wanted to be "me." Without the Asian label, I would feel better and not have any of the old negative feelings stirred up from my elementary school years.

Once again, Wilma entered my life as she wanted to join in celebrating my nuptial vows. She came to my wedding and prepared a huge feast for all the relatives. I was with a Filipina, someone that I could identify with and someone that loved me just as I was!

Seven years later, Wilma came to my home again in New York state to meet my young children. Wilma was so sweet, so tender. She treated me as if I were her own daughter. I always wondered, "Is she my mother?" I was so intrigued by that I asked her if we could travel to the Philippines together some day. However, my mother made me feel that it was not "safe" and Wilma said the trip was unaffordable. So I just continued to

Rene (center) and her daughters Jessica and Kristen.

live in America and go on with my American lifestyle of church, family, work, and friends.

After my first daughter was born, I began to get curious again and wondered about my birth parents. The face of my baby girl inspired me to want to connect with my Philippine relatives and culture. I tried to investigate, but life became very busy. Two-and-a-half years later, my second daughter was born. She looked "American" and it was at that moment that I proudly realized that I had produced both the American and Filipina look in my two lovely daughters. They represented both sides of me. My two baby girls were so beautiful. But since I did not know too much about my background, I did not engage them in dialogue about our heritage.

As I reached my forties, my mind raced with thoughts and questions. My youngest daughter, Kristen, had given me a gift to remind me that I was born in another land and to encourage me to travel and discover Manila. It was a wall canvas with a beautiful cliff and a beach in the Philippines with a note that said: "The only impossible journey is the one that you do not begin." It was my constant reminder to pray and seek out more information about Rene as a Filipina woman.

Would it be possible to travel to the Philippines? What was it like? Would I fit in? Would I be comfortable? As my curiosity peaked, I started to write letters to the place where my adoptive mother told me I was born. I began to explore how to get to the Philippines. I became enthusiastic and hopeful to find my birth mother and other relatives.

In my search for my roots and homeland, I had the opportunity to meet a few Filipinos in Hawai'i before taking my trip to the Philippines. The women I met were very kind. I felt connected and interested in them. The Filipino hospitality was second to none. The gracious welcome in my friends' homes was wonderful. There were no barriers as I was welcomed into lovely conversations. I found that Filipinos loved to chat for several hours while dining. A sisterhood was born, and I thought that these people would help me continue with my journey.

I finally went to the Philippines soon after my Hawai'i visit. It was quite an eye-opener as I had almost no memory of the landscape. It was incredible to see so many Filipino people around me. Where I grew up, I was used to being a minority figure, but here, I was surrounded by other Filipinos, all very kind souls. My first experience was a trip to Makati. It was a sprawling large city that reminded me of the big metropolitan area of New York City. I brought my daughters along so they could get a feel for their roots since, afterall, they too were of Philippine descent. We were greeted with family members and enjoyed the warm welcome. However, the people I met did not see me as a Filipino, but rather a "mestiza," someone who was of Filipino blood but exuded more of an "American look." My daughters were perceived as "pure American girls."

Since I flew to this country during my vacation, I made sure to visit the beautiful beaches of the Philippines. We went to Bohol where we travelled to the famous Chocolate Hills and to La Union, a favorite surfing spot. We went dolphin watching, zoo hiking, and sightseeing. Back in Metro Manila, the malls and the traffic were similar to American big cities. The pearl market was incredible, like a large warehouse that just went on and on with items from all over the world. At the same time, we became aware of the many poor people who lived a hand-to-mouth existence, yet who had gentle smiles. I passed by the shanties, the homes of the poor. It was truly a developing country. Though rich in natural resources, the poor abounded.

I learned some things: long meals with hours of conversation; the simple gesture of throwing toilet paper away rather than flushing it to preserve the water system. I felt uncomfortable with the language barrier, so I would just smile when addressed in Tagalog.

After 50 years of living in the United States, it is inevitable that I sit and muse over what my life would have been like if I was raised as a Filipina. I would like to reunite once again with my home away from home, but with some reservations. It is far away from the U.S., my home for all these years. I enjoy the comforts of being in America. After all, I am an American woman in a Filipina body.

Rene Brock lives in Buffalo New York. She is a literacy specialist for students in grades K-12. Rene also teaches graduate classes and tutors dyslexic students. She has two daughters and loves to spend time with them. She believes stories are man's gift to man.

Thirteen

TINIKLING THROUGH CULTURES

by Virgie Chattergy

"What race should I write on your baby's birth certificate?" the nurse asked as she stood by my bedside at the UCLA maternity ward. Without thinking, flippantly, I replied, "Human?" She wasn't amused. I was deliriously happy after a painful 16-hour labor. She was referring to the choice of either Asian or Caucasian. I asked for South East Asian, thinking that the category would include India and the Philippines. No such choice. In the pre-ethnic identity consciousness of the 1960s, racial categories were broadly defined. South East Indians were categorized as Caucasian. I chose Asian.

I remember filling out forms related to one's racial, ethnic background in those days. I would check the "other" box if there was no category for Filipino or I would check Pacific Islander. My friends would be quick to say that I should choose "Oriental" or Asian. But I believe that Filipinos are closer to being Pacific Islander. Our language and music are closer to the sounds of the Austro-Polynesian linguistic family.

While my Filipino identity unless asked, was never a big issue for me—I lean towards being global or cosmopolitan in my thinking—the Filipino "thread of life" that holds my identity, though sometimes felt thinly, never ceased to exist. As I progressed professionally and matured emotionally, that thread grew stronger. This story is about those moments and stages in

114

my life where I became aware of or was made attentive to my Filipino heritage.

I will share experiences in these different contexts of my life: growing up; being a foreign student; marrying outside of my own cultural upbringing; and, eventually, developing a career that brought me back closer to where I started—a hapa-Filipina, darting back and forth to avoid being pinched by the polarities of different cultures much like a dancer in our famous bamboo folkdance, Tinikling.

In the beginning

I was born in a tropical island of racially mixed parentage and grew up with happy memories of eating adobo, pancit, lechon, fried fish, and lots of rice, pan de sal (kind of bread) in the morning sometimes with dark tsokolate (chocolate); of running in the rain and under starlit nights; of playing all the local games with cousins and other neighborhood kids. From kindergarten through college, I attended an all-girl's English-speaking school administered and taught by Belgian nuns.

Because of this combination of a European father and Malay/Chinese mother living in a tropical island with a carefree childhood and educated by Belgians, I had no trouble relating to both Filipinos and non-Filipinos in work, in play, and in studies. I recognized differences, but they didn't matter. We had household help but that was also common at that time and helpers doing basic household cleaning, laundry, and cooking were treated fairly. Their difference in status, to me, was simply that; I never saw them as less than me except in the opportunities I had, for which I was grateful. They did things for me and I tried to do things for them in my own way, an early training of simple reciprocity or the value of utang na loob in spite of the difference in social standing.

The early messages I received from adults have left their mark. From my father: I was to become highly independent. In his words, "You were NOT born alone but will die alone and in between, you work in preparation for an independent life that will enable you to face that end." I didn't agree and told him so but he only smiled. I think I now know what he meant. He wasn't referring just to a physical aloneness (ironically, he did die alone from a massive heart attack. They found him in the bathroom early in the morning. I was in California). From my mother: "Try not to rely on others, but always be thankful when you receive help and in turn, help others. Most of all, be respectful of your elders. You owe them your life." She meant I owe her undying gratitude. From the nuns: "Let nothing come between you and God. Serve Him through serving others."

While not consciously aware of these messages from moment to moment or in day-to-day living, these tidbits of advice with their cultural underpinnings, along with many others, do manage to seep into my actions and decisions. Take teaching. I became self-reliant through teaching, a service-oriented career that began, for me, at an early age.

Initially, it was decided not by me but by the nuns who hired me at age 19 to teach kindergartners while I was still finishing my bachelor's degree in Elementary Education at the same school. At first reluctant and resistant, I gradually discovered the joyful albeit challenging task of working, playing, and learning alongside the five-year-old children.

In the mornings, I was a teacher working not just with them, but also with their parents and school administrators and colleagues. In the afternoons, I was a student; dress wear in the mornings and required student uniforms in the afternoons. Each role had different expectations.

After graduating with a BSE-Ed, I continued to teach the young ones in the mornings. In the afternoons, I taught sixth graders—quite a transition. Additionally, like other students, I volunteered to serve the community. We would visit hospitals or the poor to bring little gifts for the children, a kind of evangelization that was encouraged and valued by the nuns. Like sororities, these activities served helped form groups that were united, giving us a sense of belonging.

These experiences of having to interact and relate with different groups would serve me well when I moved to the United States. I had been navigating differences, even if poorly, for many years.

Being a Foreign Student

Until I left Cebu to pursue advanced studies at UCLA, I took my Filipino identity for granted and thought I knew all I needed to know about being Filipino. To borrow an adage, "He who only England knows, knows not England;" one cannot really know one's country until he knows another with which to compare and contrast. Until I married a fellow foreign student from India, I didn't know how another person could regard what I consider fundamental aspects of life so differently.

Even more fundamental are these questions: How did I even get it into my head to leave a successful teaching career in the Philippines and venture into becoming a student all over again on foreign soil? How was it possible that, having been a president of a Student Catholic Action group at an all-girls private school administered and managed by Belgian sisters, I could comfortably get married and stay married to a Hindu-raised gentleman?

I wondered out loud over these recently. Said my older son in reply, "Because you are like that tikling bird who jumps between pole to keep from being hurt and pinned down. From the start, Mom, you have always been living on two levels or two cultures. Think about it."

I now realize that my bicultural existence which began at birth, extended throughout my early education, through graduate studies, married life, and a career that encouraged even further my understanding of how two cultures can meet, negotiate, and compromise in order to co-exist for the benefit of both.

There were things that surprised, and other things that I adjusted and adapted to easily in the five years and two months that I lived in Los Angeles, where I completed a master of arts and doctoral degrees in Education. In the first year, I completed a Certificate Program in Teaching English as a Second Language. My interest in the TESL program was piqued while attending two summer classes at Philippine Normal College in Manila where adjunct teaching members from the UCLA program were visiting instructors. By the end of the second summer session, I decided that going through the entire program instead of just taking two or three courses made more sense.

It was in that first year that I needed to factor into a class project my natal culture and language. A representative from each of the 22 countries represented in the project were asked to say something about their place of origin. Fortunately for me, there was a remarkably bright Filipina from Manila who spoke passionately and knowledgeably about the Philippines. She spoke for us both!

A growing awareness regarding my Filipino identity began to take shape partly because of professors' and peers' expectations of me and largely because I knew that the better I understood who I was, where I came from, and what I believed in, the better I would be able to handle the uncertainties that adapting to a different environment brings. Self-knowledge, for me, has always served as an anchor. My strategies included interacting with other Filipino students on campus, meeting members of the Filipino community, and reading up on aspects of Philippine culture.

Through all these, I found myself sometimes in agreeable companionship with others, but at other times, I seemed to be thinking/acting outside the circle of Filipino normative and acceptable behaviors. For instance, take the use of the go-between. I was in conversation with a Filipino friend (A) when her friend (B) came over to join us at a party. My friend introduced us and B started asking questions about me, while periodically glancing in my direction with a genuine inviting smile:

> B: When did Virgie come to the States?

> A: She recently arrived and is taking classes at UCLA.

> B: Oh, where is she from in the Philippines? Single, *ba*?

> A: Galing sa (from) Cebu and yes, single. Do you know of any good-looking man she can meet?

> B: Ay, wala, pero (no but) I will keep my eyes open for her. Ano bang klasing lalaki ang gusto niya (what kind of guy does she like)? And how long is she staying?

Completely bewildered about why she was asking about me in my presence, which was disconcerting, I barged in. "Why don't you ask me instead of A?" And so she did.

On the surface, this seems very trivial but further readings and discussions on Filipino values have given me an insight into the underlying reason for this behavior. I was at that point ibang-tao (other) to her even though she made me feel welcomed. So important is being sensitive to other people's feelings and so careful not to offend, Filipinos will first try to find out who and what one should know before speaking directly to a new acquaintance. Hence the use of third parties. Using an indirect as opposed to an "in-your-face" approach is not only polite but desirable. Especially in relation to an authority figure, a person in a subordinate position will usually use a third party.

Flash forward. While overseeing a federally funded fellowship program that focused on cultural and language differences in the classroom at the University of Hawai'i at Manoa, I assisted teachers with a good number of newly arrived immigrant students from the Philippines. A teacher asked, "Why does Carmen (fictitious name) always speak for Norma? One day, Carmen asked if Norma could go to the comfort room (restroom) and can she go with her?" While not all Filipinos

119

subscribe to this behavior, the overall feeling of a sense of comfort to have a spokesperson is not uncommon.

Although I've never used a go-between, I have personally experienced cultural differences regarding respect for authority. Such behavior as not looking a person of higher status directly in the eye as a sign of respect stayed with me even up to my early years as an assistant professor. The practice ended the day my department chair covered the papers on her desk while talking to me. She thought I was trying to read her papers. Nothing was farther from my mind. Nevertheless, legitimate respect for authority is a value I support. It hasn't always been easy for me as I tend to question rules and the excessive wielding of power by authority figures.

The importance of smooth social interactions for Filipinos cannot be overestimated. Although establishing (and maintaining) relationships is a universally desirable behavior, its emphasis and influence on social behaviors differ from one culture to the next. To a Filipino, social relationships are a primary consideration, so much so that sociologists, Filipinos and non-Filipinos, have recognized it as identifiably Filipino. Virgilio Enriquez, a Filipino social scientist, and his team have identified eight levels and types of relationships, ranging from the most impersonal with least involvement, pakikitungo (civility), to pakikiisa (full trust). I identify with some of these and find our system of relationships admirable, although sometimes confusing and at times intrusive.

Cross-Racial/Cultural Marriage

Speaking of rules, one cardinal offense from the perspective of my Catholic upbringing was to marry outside of the faith. That's exactly what I did. My justification was the teaching that everyone is a child of God. Why not Rahul? As a friend noted, the nuns would have approved of him—a well-educated, good and kindly, responsible, serious, and honest fellow, except that not only was he not Catholic, he was not even

Virgie and her Chattergy family.

Christian! Ah, but precisely because he wasn't Christian that I feared no conflict about which tradition to follow. He was a non-practicing Hindu and generally, Hindus don't proselytize. The hari-Krishna movement was created by the West and faddish. Furthermore, he took the required Cana pre-marriage classes and promised not to get in the way of my Catholic practices, which he actually encouraged. I was very comfortable with East Indians because my best friend in Cebu was from Southern India. She considered me her sister or some close relation in her past life.

Of all the men I dated while studying at UCLA, Rahul attracted me on many levels. Headstrong as I have always been, I believed that our differences in upbringing and temperament wouldn't be a serious barrier. No one approved of this union. But 52 years later, I was at his side throughout his short illness, and with our two sons thanked him for his love before he was laid to rest. Difficult years? Very. Insurmountable? No. I was taught that love was ultimately in the will; he was taught about commitments.

Perseverance, resilience, and the idea that suffering is part of living were ingrained in both of us—he, through his Asian upbringing and me as a Filipino. Personally, I don't believe that we are meant to suffer in this life. If and when we do, it is our own doing though we cannot always understand, nor control the factors that lead to it. "The fault, Brutus, is not in our stars, but in ourselves".

It would take another book to explore, reflect, and tease out the nuances expressed in cross-cultural or mixed racial marriages. For now, it is enough to say that, during that stage in my life, there was a lot of dancing between more than two poles to avoid irreparable damage to my toes. The same can be said about Rahul's experiences living with a tikling bird. He would say it is his karma. However, there were silver linings through it all.

Coming Full Circle

I have Rahul to thank for choosing the University of Hawai'i instead of Syracuse where he had also received an offer to be an assistant professor. He believed that in Hawai'i we would be closer to Asia if we wanted to visit home and the "people environment" was more familiar. It is here in Hawai'i where about 25 percent of the population is Filipino, that I came face to face with my cultural identity. Interacting, advising, and being in constant contact with Filipinos of all ages in different settings, slowly but consistently held up a mirror for me and helped clarify and get me re-acquainted with my roots.

From the children, I was reminded often of the young Filipinos' respectful approach to authority and their reticence to speak up unless asked. My student, Joey Pablo, conducted a study about how teachers respond to relatively newly arrived Filipino students' call for help. To ask for help, the children used eye contact, followed by a shy smile when the teacher looked directly at them or quickly looked down at the desk. In a school culture where talk is valued, these children were at a disadvantage. "Children are seen, not heard" is the rule in the early formation of their character in the Philippines. What was functional in their upbringing became dysfunctional in this school setting.

Pablo's conclusion described three patterns of teacher responses. One type of teacher said they saw the non-verbal look for help, but "when in Rome, do as the Romans;" another type of teacher said, "I noticed the non-verbal call for help, but by the time I got around to the end of the class, I'd forgotten;" the third type of teacher said, "What look?" Hence the need for cross-cultural workshops!

I found this instructive and enlightening. In contrast, I don't remember being intimidated and spoke up in class readily. I also remember, however, that I was never a teacher's pet. I attribute my boldness to my being hapa—of mixed blood though I wasn't alone in this behavior in class as far as other Filipino classmates were concerned. Nevertheless, what stands out in my generation was the value of being respectful before authorities and looking them in the eye was considered rude.

From my own students, I benefited from having a group of dedicated, committed, and loyal Filipinos among the ethnically diverse cohort. I complemented their formal studies with informal get-togethers outside of the university setting. These socials bonded them, brought out their generosity of spirit, flare for cooking, and love of music and dancing. Out came the traditional songs, the bamboo sticks, the stories and most of all, the home cooking that brought nostalgia for some.

I believe love of music is in a Filipino's DNA. Even the Spaniards logged their admiration of the Filipino's innate musical talent. One does not have to be on stage or expensively tutored. Most Filipinos can burst into song in a social setting. This is only surpassed by the affinity for food, and sharing. Everyone in the fellowship program completed their studies. The program offered them a scaffolding to move out of temporary status to tenure track positions in the Department of Education. Friendships continued long after the program was over. Relationships count.

Given my position in the University, I was often invited to speak on the subject of Philippine history and culture. Often colleagues wondered at how diverse we are from Aparri to Jolo. To do justice to these discussions, I had to read up on our past to explain the commonalities and differences with other cultures—things I missed learning about in my own early years of schooling. As an archipelago, composed of several islands and separated by coastlines and mountain ranges, languages and traditions, the Philippines has much to offer to other island communities, Mainland USA, and the world. And Filipinos have lots to learn and gain from knowing and living in other cultural environments. Filipinos can do that because, for the most part, they are noted to be resilient.

My journey through life, starting with being bilingual/bicultural, has enriched me. In retirement, there has been less need to jump between the poles as I settle down to realize I am whole—a Filipina.

Virgie Chattergy is a professor and assistant dean emeritus of the University of Hawai'i at Manoa, College of Education. She lives in Honolulu with her two sons and two grandsons. Dr. Chattergy continues to be active as a docent at the Honolulu Museum of Art which houses the largest Philippine Gallery in the country. She received her M.A. and ED.d from UCLA and a BSE-Ed from St. Theresa's Cebu.

Fourteen

BLESSED ARE THE BILINGUALS

By Josephine Dicsen Pablo

How many languages can you speak? How did you learn to speak "good" English? How did you learn to read and write in English?

I was asked these questions when I came to Hawai'i in 1968 when I applied at the State Department of Education (DOE) for a teaching position.

My answer to the first question: Ilocano, Tagalog, English, Spanish. To the second—learning "good" English meaning Standard English (grammar-based)—I said, "In the elementary public schools, and private schools in high school and college." I gave the same answer to the third question.

Some people outside the Philippines are unaware that English is the medium of instruction in public and private schools in the country. Before the Americans came, Spanish was the medium of instruction for a few elite. During World War II, Japanese was taught. I became bilingual or multilingual growing up. It was a natural, painless process.

I was the eldest girl of four children. My mom, who is from, Aringay, La Union, spoke Ilocano, and my dad, who is from Benguet, Mt. Provinces, spoke Inibaloy, Ilocano, and English. I was born in Baguio City, Benguet, Mt. Province, where the majority of the residents spoke Ilocano and English.

As early as five or six years old, I was reading in English. I read the Golden Book series over and over until I could memorize a whole book from cover to cover. At the same time, I borrowed from neighbors and domestic helpers the Ilocano magazine, *Bannawag,* and the Pilipino magazine, *Liwayway.*

I attended a pilot school in elementary grades where English was the medium of instruction, while Ilocano was spoken in the playground. I bought and/or borrowed Tagalog comics (i.e., *Hiwaga,* Tagalog *Klasiks*) and enjoyed reading comics in English like Popeye, Tarzan, Three Musketeers, and others. It was my second-grade teacher, Miss Rimando, who "discovered" my writing skills (cursive) by posting my work on the "Best Work" Bulletin. In the fifth and sixth grades, my Tagalog oral, reading, and writing proficiencies increased with classroom activities like recitation of poems, riddles, rhymes, songs, simulated radio broadcasting, skits, essay writing, and spelling contests. By high school through college, I became more proficient in English and Tagalog than I was with Ilocano.

Being bilingual got me my first teaching job at the Hawai'i Department of Education (DOE). I was hired initially for a federally funded temporary position as a bilingual aide in 1975. As a bilingual aide, my job was to assist the regular teacher with instruction for non- and limited-English speaking students. I increased my proficiency in Ilocano on the job since I was also asked to translate instructional materials. In one-and-a-half years, I became a field demonstrator (resource teacher), developing, field testing, and disseminating Ilocano-English bilingual materials for grades K-3 Language Arts and Math.

Finally in 1978, I qualified for an educational officer position, providing technical assistance to ensure equal educational opportunity to immigrant students who were labeled English Language Learners (ELLs).

It was understood that I was to promote Bilingual Education in contrast to English as a Second Language (ESL). In

1975, Hawai'i DOE received a federal grant to demonstrate a Transitional Bilingual Education Project. This type of project develops English language proficiency through the initial use of native language for instruction. I used myself as living proof of the success of such an approach/model.

In an effort to make the ELLs learn how to speak English, regular classroom teachers often discourage the use of the native language at home. Parents are told to use English only "so their children will speak and learn in English," thus, creating a generational communication gap between parents, grandparents, and children. This, sadly, has resulted in language loss not only among local Filipinos, but also among other groups (e.g. Japanese, Hawaiians). Someone once wrote that "to lose a language is to lose a culture."

In Hawai'i, tri-lingual Filipino nuns assigned to the Kalihi and Waipahu area were told by parents to use standard English only for instruction. The parents were concerned that that their children would acquire Filipino accents and/or will not understand instruction. Experience and research have shown that accent is not transferrable and has no significant effect on academic performance.

In 1995-97, I wrote a language enhancement project patterned after the Kamehameha Preschool Hawaiian Immersion model. Project Keiki (Child) was an alternative instructional project mainly for pre-K students. Parents participated actively in the classroom and provided native language support together with bilingual teachers. In addition, ESL instruction was provided for both students and parents.

Project Keiki proved that preschool children who are taught in their home language achieve better and learn English faster in kindergarten. In my closing remarks at a bilingual conference, I restated the project objective, "the use of the native language at home and in school," and cited research and the final evaluation results of the project. Our native language connects us with our culture, our identity, our values, and traditions. If we lose it, we lose something of ourselves, of what we can be.

As mentioned earlier, during my job interview for the teaching position, one of the interviewers asked where and how I learned to speak English. Apparently, I did not have a "Filipino accent" like the other applicants from the Philippines. After a decade of living in Hawaiʻi, a German lady friend said I had a German accent. Often, language is heard from the perspective of the listener.

Bilingual education for both students and teachers.

After graduate school from the University of Hawaiʻi at Manoa, I was invited to make an oral presentation of my master's thesis ("Coping Behavior Patterns of Students of Limited English Proficiency in a Classroom," 1980) to a group of school administrators from the U.S. Mainland. After my talk, a school superintendent approached and complemented me for a job well done. He then added, "You have an accent;" to which I answered with a smile, "You too. Texan?" He nodded and asked, "Filipino?" I asked, "How do you know?" He answered, "I was in the military and stationed there during the war" and added something in Tagalog. I was quite impressed. I answered him in Tagalog and added in English, "I love my accent."

Whenever I hear somebody mention accents, I would say, "Lucky you have an accent, that means you are bilingual." Some of our newly arrived students from the Philippines hesitate or refrain from speaking English even if they can speak it because of their accent. Remarks like, "you talk funny; can't understand what you are saying; talk slowly," can be discouraging. As a result, they can read or write better than they can speak.

Filipino vowel sounds (a e i o u) are similar to Hawaiian. Grammatically, we interchange the use of he/she because in Ilocano and Tagalog, there is one personal pronoun for both genders. The interchange between the *f* to *p* sounds are common.

Even non-verbal behaviors can be misunderstood or be confusing and may affect academic development. Newly arrived professionals such as doctors, teachers, lawyers, engineers, and nurses have experienced embarrassing, sometimes humorous communication gaps leading to brief employment or loss of self-esteem. In the early plantation days, negative stereotypes resulted due to wrong interpretation of manong/manang, terms of respect for authority or elderly. To counter such stereotype, Filipino students from UH Manoa formed the Operation Manong Program.

When I arrived in Hawai'i in 1968, I was expecting the residents to be speaking in Hawaiian. To my disappointment, I only heard Hawaiian in song and hula. My exposure to the Hawaiian language occurred during a teacher orientation at a Catholic private school where I was hired to teach math and science in the intermediate grades. In addition to the usual information about the school philosophy and policies, we were given a list of "must know" Hawaiian words and practiced their correct pronunciation: Hawai'i, aloha, mahalo, ohana, pau, hana, pua, keiki, kapu, ewa, wai, makai, mauka.

My two children born here speak the local Pidgin in spite of the fact that we spoke Ilocano and standard English at home. At first, I was concerned this might affect their grades in language arts (i.e., reading and writing). A linguist and ESL professor once wrote that low test scores in standardized test may be affected by Pidgin. But the children did well in school.

Later, I met and befriended another linguist and ESL professor who taught Pidgin or Hawai'i Creole English (HCE) at UH Manoa. I became interested in Pidgin. I read the "Pidgin to the Max" comics; attended a few sessions at the university; and even took the Hana Bata test, a proficiency test in Pidgin. I failed!

I did not intend to be able to speak Pidgin but wanted to know how it affects academic achievement in reading and writing. Once I found out that HCE is considered a language and not a dialect, I became excited about the possibility of a bilingual Pidgin/HCE and English program.

Project Akamai (smart) received federal funds with a high score in the "Need for Project" criterion. Data showed that three quarters of the Hawai'i student population are Pidgin/HCE speakers. Under the project, HCE was used in Social Studies and Science followed by ESL approaches. At the end of five years, grades 9-12 HCE speakers acquired standard English and did better in the two content areas.

In the Philippines, the use of "carabao" (water buffalo) English, a kind of pidgin, is acceptable. It is common to mix languages in a social conversation. A few examples are: "You go digus na (go take a bath already)" or, "Go bring out the basura (trash)." Taglish, a combination of Tagalog and English is popular. "Oy, how sweet naman!. (Wow, how sweet it is)!" and "pakikuenta mo nga how much (can you estimate/compute how much)?"

Is it possible to forget or lose a language once learned? Yes, if not spoken regularly. A real example is Father Sal (not his real name). Newly ordained, he was assigned to work in Brazil. For 15 years, he did not have anybody to converse with in Ilocano. English was spoken among the priests in the religious community. He learned Portuguese, the language of the local community. When he came back from his mission, he apologized for not speaking in Ilocano. This phenomenon known as language atrophy happens when the language is not used for a period of time especially as one grows older.

After retirement, I visited my late father's home village in Datacan, Benguet to attend a relative's wedding. During the nuptial mass, the Korean pastor gave his homily in Inibaloy, the community dialect; Ilocano, the dominant language spoken; and English. It was quite impressive since he had been assigned there only two years prior. His homily was short and sweet, a clear, meaningful, and spirit-filled sermon. It was heartwarming to hear the familiar sounds of Inibaloy that I learned when I was four or five years old. Now, I am relearning the language from my nieces through cell phone text messages and video chats.

My hope is that my children and their children's children learn at least three languages other than English—Ilocano, Tagalog, and Spanish, the major languages of Filipino-Americans in California, where they now reside.

We live in a multicultural, global society, with more possibilities and opportunities to develop and enrich our humanness and well-being. Be multilingual and be thankful for your ability to speak two or more languages...for you can have the best of many worlds.

Josephine Dicsen Pablo, M.A. (Science Education), M.Ed. (Curriculum & Instruction with emphasis in Multicultural Education). A resident of Mililani, Hawai'i, Joey is originally from Baguio City and was an instructor at St. Louis University before coming to Hawai'i in 1968. She worked as an educational specialist at the Office of Instructional Services of the Hawai'i State Department of Education (DOE). After retiring in 2000, she served as educational consultant for the Program for English Language Learners and part-time instructor for the Outreach College, College of Education, University of Hawai'i.

Fifteen

PAGSASAULA SA WIKANG PAMBANSA

by Nilda Boland

This poem is written with passion and fury in the national language or wikang pambansa after the author read that politician Teodoro Locsin, Jr. disparaged the use of Tagalog/Pilipino. An English translation follows.

Di ako mapakali,
Gusto kitang sabunutan!
Di ko maubos maisip
Balang araw mahagip ng aking mata
At makabasa ng mga salitang
Hihimay sa kalamnan ng pagiging makabayan.

Di mapakali
At parang my sumusundot
Sa 'yong salumpupuwit.
Lumakad pabalik-balik
At di alam kung bakit.
Kumunot ang noo
At nagmumurang mag-isa
Para kang sinaktan
Na wala naming nanghambalos.
Binalikan mo ulit at binasa
Ang dahilan ng iyong pagbabalisa
Sa pangalawang pagkakataon
Dapat ka ngang maging balisa!

132

Siya nga!
At binabalahura ang pambansang wika
Na iyong minahal
At maagang ginamit
Sa pag akda ng mga tulang naging kaagapay
Sa panahong ika'y nag-iisa
At kailangang maisakataga ang mga paghihirap ng kalooban
Na kung hindi mailapat sa papel na parisukat
Ika'y animong sasambulat
Na may maaring masaktan
O ikaw ay mapariwara.
Wikang Pilipino ang nag antabay
Upang ang galit ay hanggang salita lamang
Gamit ang tinta at papel.

At para na ring sinalaula mo ang aking guro
Sa asignaturang Pilipino
Sa mataas na paaralan ng lungsod ng Cavite.

Mas madali sana kitang napatawad
Kahit kapit-tuko ka man kay Duterte
Subalit kung pati pambansang wika ay iyo nang yinurakan
Mula ngayon,
Mukha at apelyido mo pa lang
Ay lalagyan ko na ng krokis
At tatandaang ika'y mapait pa sa apdo
Ng sawang kumakain ng sarili nyang laman-loob.

Mananalaytay sa aking iwing pakiramdam
Tuwing ika'y dadaan
Sa aking mapanurin'g mata
Kapag ang wikang Filipino ang hinahaliparot.

Mabuti pa sa'yo ang isda na may angking langsa
Lagyan lang ng luya ay mapaparam.
Subalit ikaw,

Oo, ikaw!
Di malulusaw ang kasalanang pag alipusta
Sa sariling wika
Ilubog ka man sa kumukulong asupre.

Ganun pa man salamat sa galit
Na dulot ng iyong kawalang-modo
Ako ay nakahabi ng tula
Kakayahang matagal na naisantabi
Danga't kasi'y walang mahagilap na inspirasyon
Dito sa mundong magulo
At punong-puno ng mga nilalang na katulad mo.
Nangaglipana sa kapaligiran
At naghihintay ng tamang andas
Upang maghari
Palakpakan at ipagbunyi
Ng may kaparehong sungay.

Sila ay maaring nagdidiwang sa ngayon
Habang tayo ay nanggalaiti sa galit.
Lumayas ka kaya sa bayang Pilipinas Teddy Boy Locsin!
Ang iyong paa at lupang sinilangan
Ay di magkatugma.
Hindi ka karapa-dapat
Manapa'y ika'y naliligaw!

Kung kaya't aking itutuloy
Ang aking panggagalaiti
Kinabukasang nagising
Na may bahid pa rin ng pagtatanong.

May katuturan bang magdiwang?
Kahirap maglubid ng mga kataga
Kung ang pinatutungkulan mong bansa
Ay niluluray ng mga nakaupong timawa
Na malugod na iniluluklok

Ng mamamayang dalita at salat sa pang-unawa.

Kabayan, kelan ka ba talaga mamumulat?
Kaylan aalisin ang piring ng kamangmangan?
Anong klaseng aralin ang aakma sa kupad ng utak
Upang alamin na ang iyong dukhang kalagayan
Ay kayo rin ang may akda?

Ilang pag diriwang pa kaya ng kalayaan
Ang ating palilipasin
Upang umusbong sa puso
At amining tayo ay marangal
May paninindigan, ginagalang, masipag, masayahin,
Mahilig makipagsapalaran,
Subalit sa sariling bakuran ay burara'ng nakahilata.
Mahirap bang maging Pilipino?
O mananatili bang hanggang katanungan na lang?
O bansang sawi,
Sandamakmak mang bayani ang ating ialay
Ni sa panaginip tayo ay di pa rin magmamalay!
Mananatiling duhagi magpakailanman!

(Araw ng mga Bayani, 2020)

PROSTITUTING THE NATIONAL LANGUAGE

I cannot be still, I want to pull your hair
Cannot understand why I have to see and read by chance,
Mean words that pick the flesh of a patriot.

I cannot be still as if something irked my butt
Walking back and forth knew nothing of the reason
Creased the forehead and cursed to myself
As if tormented by somebody where there's none
Reread it to know what made me angry
And sure enough, it's you!

Yes, it's you! You're the one!
He that doesn't respect the motherland's tongue, the one that
you love most by heart,

One used to pen a poem that gave company in time of aloneness
That burdened the soul when the words have to be written on a
piece of paper.
When one feels about to explode, that some may get hurt or may
perish,
That language so patiently waits
So that the anger only stays as words using pen and paper.

And as if you insulted my high school Filipino teacher in Cavite
City.
I would have forgiven you easily even if you tightly cling to
Duterte's clout
But since you spit on the national language, from now on I
promise myself
To see your face and name randomly, I'll mark an x and
remember
That you are a snake with bitter liver, a boa that eats its own
innards.
Fish is better that you with its distinct smell

Cook it with ginger and smell no more.
But you! Yes you!
The stigma will stay even if you are submerged in boiling sulphur.

Nevertheless, thank you for the anger
The talent I thought I have, unused for lack of inspiration
In this chaotic world peopled by the likes of you
Among the hordes of masses, waiting to be celebrated and anointed
Because you all have horns.

You may be celebrating by now, whilst others are annoyed to the bones,
Why don't you just leave the Philippines, Teddy Boy Locsin.
Your feet do not belong to the ground you are stepping on
You do not deserve to be here, you do not belong
So maybe I can go sleep and wake up tomorrow
Not harboring the same question I have, before closing my eyes.

Why do we have to celebrate when it's hard to tie words
If the country you are dedicating it to
Is being shredded by the ruling crocs
The masses themselves willingly elected them to power.

Countrymen, when are we going to be aware, when to remove the blindfolds?
What apt education can hasten our learning
And claim that the lowly life and poverty around us, is our own making?

How many more celebrations of freedom to watch and partake
And know that we are decent people, respectful, determined, know hard work
Easy to laugh and are adventurous.
But in our land sometimes we do not care.

Is it hard to be a Filipino? Or will this just remain to be a question mark?

O my country of birth!

How many more heroes we have to offer to jolt us into reality.

Or let it stay as dreams and be exploited forever.

Nilda Laurio Boland *is the youngest of eight children who were orphaned early in life. She started writing poetry at 12 to drown out life's struggles. Her first husband was gunned down and she was incarcerated for a year during Martial Law. She ran a preschool while working as a community organizer before immigrating to Hawai'i.*

Sixteen

QUADRIPTYCH
Four Women Rediscover Pinay Identity

by Fe Lucero Baran, Coco, Johanna and Cat

Scrolling through Etsy as I sometimes do in my retirement life, a stunning life-sized quadriptych painting by Romanian artist Pataki-Barothi in San Anselmo, California caught my eye. Depicting four women in identical facial expressions but each in varied shades of color, with flowing intertwining hair and gauzy shimmering attire, they represent The Four Seasons: spring, summer, fall and winter. My mind wandered from the women in the painting to the four women of my own family and our memories of our Filipino heritage.

As an octogenarian living in Pismo Beach, California, I am winter with the coolness of pale grey and the lightness in soft blue colors from head to toe. A widow since 2012, I am the mother of three women. My first daughter, Coco in the fall colors of fiery reds and magentas with some gold, again from head to toe; the second, Johanna in her golden summer colors of green, blue, pink, and magenta with some gold and green; and the third, Cat, in her spring monochromatic hues of green, greenish blue, and pink. It is as if we are the four women in the painting, intertwined from one panel to another, either looking on each other or away from another, detachable from each other as polyptych paintings are, yet connected to each other.

The Baran women (l to r): Johanna from Pismo Beach, Coco from Los Angeles, Fe, and Cat from Millersville, Maryland.

As I sat contemplating my family in light of the artwork, I wondered what each daughter's perspective would be of Filipino or Filipina culture. I asked them their thoughts about how Filipino culture shaped them and would like to share them here.

Winter: *First Generation Rediscoveries*

Fe Lucero Baran

As a World War II baby, I was born in 1941, a couple of weeks after the bombing of Pearl Harbor and a month before the defeat of Filipino and American forces in Manila. Living my childhood in a farm south of Cebu City, close to the earth and far from the occupying Japanese, I was oblivious to the adults whispering about relatives imprisoned by the invading forces, and later the far away Bataan Death March and the Filipino-American defeat in Corregidor. Barely four when Corregidor, the gateway to Manila, was retaken by American forces, I heard the victorious celebration and thanksgiving when the War officially ended in September 1945.

The traditional cultural values inculcated in this era and the next decade were steeped in family especially respect for elders, developing and keeping mutual friendships whether at home or at school, educational excellence in the mastery of English and Pilipino, and the pursuit of religious and spiritual practices. These paradigms shaped my life and must have seeped through to my daughters one way or another.

Young and fearless in the historic 1960s, amidst another war in Vietnam, Laos, and Cambodia, and on my way to graduate school at the University of California in Los Angeles, I attended an anthropology orientation course at the Ateneo University in Quezon City. The then-leading anthropologists, Frank Lynch, SJ and Mary Hollensteiner, taught that understanding the differences between Filipino and American world views was essential in adjusting to the new culture. The buzz words were personalistic Filipino compared to mechanistic American, so I boiled it down to "it's not personal, it's business" or its "either personalistic or individualistic."

What is dualistic is the phenomenon that even business in Filipino terms is always personal. It was my business to pass my courses to fulfill an obligation to family and sponsors; get along to make new friends in a foreign country, often at one's personal expense; to keep the faith; connect with family; be grateful, generous and not cause any hiya (shame or embarrassment). All in all, I knew and understood the American culture and stereotypes more than the Americans did mine, so this was and still is the secret to a happy assimilation and compromise.

In the process of education as my business, I discovered that Americans can be personal too but in a more direct fashion. For instance, in response to an invitation, there's the literal meaning of American "yes or no," and the Filipino tentative, deemed polite "maybe or I will see/try." If it's a date, the American eventually thinks or asks, "You're not sure?" In the meantime, Filipinos, as much as they want to say "yes," deal with an ingrained obligation to ask permission or tell parents first, or the admonition to beware of foreigners. It is an interesting linguistic and cultural difference.

Living in the U.S. as an immigrant, marrying a Polish American and raising children in the 1970's was more of a challenge than attending school. Raising three girls required work, a new way of planning and seeing things, and solving problems not addressed in graduate classrooms. Soon we realize that as immigrants, struggling with keeping old habits, building new ones, then deciding which are the positive ones become crucial because according to Gandhi, habits become our destiny.

James Clear reminds us in "Atomic Habits" that the ultimate purpose of habits or automatic behavior is to solve the problems of life with as little energy as possible. Ironically, identifying and revising habits are not easy nor clear. For me, it wasn't always easy to reprimand kids, especially other kids, or explain to the teacher or principal why your child was doing one thing and not another. Often lost in translation are endearing words like "I love you" to my children, since there are no equivalent words in Cebuano except palanga, which means "dear one" or, in Pilipino, mahal kita meaning "You are dear to me." After raising three daughters and having been married for 42 years, one realizes many new habits, practiced in small doses, did make life easier.

As I have evolved in the past 50 years, the world too has changed. It has become smaller and many cultural traits have become universal. In the U.S. for instance, cultural diversity leads to more freedom and tolerance (or so we hope). Every generation has to discover ways that make life easier or more productive while keeping what one values.

Filipino families generally still cling to the idea of a closely knit family, living together, or supporting each other even when apart. Kimberly Ellis of Family Watch International, in her book "The Invincible Family," encourages us to trust that the family, as the fundamental unit of society, will be impossible to crush entirely because it is self-generating and has existed long before dynasties, governments, or political factions.

Fall: *A Simple Life*

Coco Baran

My Mother was so vibrant and active in her youth and young adulthood. She was a proficiently trained pianist. I saw her pictures in old albums when I visited the Philippines. She once told me that her father, my Lolo, Papa Tiago, wanted her to study medicine. But since he had five other children, he forgot his plan for her. As a result, instead of medicine, she was off to another country on a Fulbright scholarship. She ended up studying "Teaching English as a Second Language" at UCLA.

When I was an unhappy teenager and trying to find my own path in life, she said to me that "life was so simple" for her growing up. All she did was "pray and study." I had often wondered about that. Pray, study, and live a simple life. Hmmm… That was very interesting and I thought about that for many years to come. Forty years later I am still thinking about it.

When I was a baby, we moved from Cebu in the Philippines to Seattle, Washington. My Polish/American father, who met my mother in the Philippines, had work lined up in the U.S. I went to Catholic school and we went to mass every Sunday. So far, like my mom's youth, I was praying, studying, and living a "simple life." It started to change from simple to complicated when my mom insisted that I try out for the school talent show. Ummmm…

Coco leads the dancing prisoners of Cebu.

Like in mom's simple life, I studied piano. The apple didn't fall far from the tree. And now, she wanted me to share my talent with the world. Each year, she insisted that I try out for the school talent show (and sing too). Yup, sing while playing the piano.

The first year, my piece was "Peter, Peter, Pumpkin Eater." The next year was "When the Moon was Rocking." And every year, the talent show judges selected me to be in the show. After years of piano, mom changed it up.

She insisted that I perform Filipino folk dances. I was so embarrassed. Now, this was asking too much! The mean kids made fun of my number, Itik-Itik (The Duck Dance). But, even though some of my classmates and the eighth grade bullies teased me on the playground, the applause was resounding after every show! I cannot tell you how much I hated doing this for my mom. But it's all right, in retrospect. I don't regret it now.

Ironically, despite my embarrassment, I did go on for the rest of my life as a dancer and actor. Years later, in a Hollywood, California acting class, I met other Filipinos and they all said that their moms insisted that they sing and dance for everyone too! Music and dance are in our genes.

I was invited in Cebu to perform with the dancing inmates of Cebu at CPDRC. Filipinos' gravitation to music and dance truly unites us as one symbiotic culture. It is even spiritual for Filipinos. During the Sinulog festival in Cebu, close to two million people come for nonstop dancing to honor Cebu's Santo Niño. We can celebrate our Filipino mothers with the simple life of prayer, study, music...and dance. Afterall, my simple life of prayer and study led to dancing pathways and cadences of rhythm and rapture. In conclusion, my Filipino mother passed on to me the beautiful traits of being Filipino, which is reflected in the beauty of the land. Mabuhay to our mothers and mabuhay ang Pilipinas!

Summer:

Three Powerful Strengths I Learned from my Filipina Mom

Johanna Baran Moore

My parents immigrated to the United States before I was born, and I was raised in Seattle in an American multicultural family. I can remember feeling unique compared to my friends whose parents grew up and lived in this country, mostly because of my physical features. Even today, people commonly ask me what nationality or ethnicity I am, finding it difficult to put me in

145

Summer family: Michael, Max, Fe, Mia, and Johanna.

a distinct group. Maybe it's because of the mix of my father's Polish side and my mother's Filipino side, which is an added layer to the combination of Chinese, Spanish, and American influences already found within Filipinos.

Although my face reflects a diverse lineage, as a child I didn't feel like I came from an ethnic or distinctly cultural household. My mother does have a slight accent, but I didn't notice it much as a child. Going to visit Filipino family in the United States or Canada, to Filipino festivals, or the Philippines only enforced the feeling that I was much more American than Filipino, and certainly not Polish! I didn't speak Tagalog, never learned the Tinikling bamboo pole dances or the Itik-Itik duck dance; the only Filipino food I knew of was lumpia and rice (and Coca Cola).

I avoided karaoke like my life depended on it, and once when I wore a Filipino folk dress with the butterfly sleeves, I felt VERY out of place. Visiting Filipino families and going to Filipino parties was always fun because Filipinos are so friendly, love to laugh, dance, and tell jokes, but that was not a part of my typical family life. Although there were many Filipino stereotypes that I didn't see myself fitting into, looking back on my youth, I see that more subtle but powerful aspects of my mother's Filipino culture were deeply ingrained in our family and in me.

Much of the success I've experienced is directly related to my mother's influence. My mother is an intelligent, hardworking, curious woman who is kind, joyful, and generous. As a child, I interpreted her quiet, calm demeanor as subservience in a culture where people were constantly trying to assert themselves. But I now realize that she was quietly reigning over everyone as the matriarch, just as her mother did before her. It was only later in life when I met other successful Filipina women, that I realized the strength, patient intelligence, and strict expectations set for us by our mothers. Three Filipina characteristics that have contributed to my success are restraint, diligence, and compassion.

Diligence. My mother taught at the local community college and despite having small children, commuting long miles, and running a household with a traveling father, she always prepared and followed up for her students. I can remember her stacks of worksheets laying around in not-so-neat piles, books everywhere, and my mother, in the midst of it all, grading papers late into the evenings after dinner was over and dishes were done. Partly by example and partly by the subtle and silent look and body language that only mothers can give, I realized that I was expected to work hard and with consistency.

Restraint. The tourist in the shop told her daughter no, and her daughter stamped her feet and furiously raised her voice. Her mother matched her tone and the two went toe to toe, ending in the girl in full blown tantrum on the floor and the mother fuming. My heart went out to both parties, and I wanted to pass the mother a note that says, "I know. I'm a mom too." I remember my mother telling me a similar story about one of these scenarios in the Philippines, and she too felt terrible for both parties, but also horrified to be a witness in the store. For my mother, controlling, or at least hiding, emotions is key. Her stoicism and strength are immense, and certainly her actions have influenced my own ability to stay cool under pressure, at least for a period of time.

Compassion. One Filipino trait that I can relate to is dedication to the Catholic Church. Even trips away from home did not preclude Sunday morning mass, as we would drive around unfamiliar towns on Saturday looking for mass schedules to coordinate into our trip itinerary. To this day, my mother will pass an envelope with cash to me in the middle of mass, as it is the child's responsibility to drop the envelope into the basket as it passes from pew to pew.

I always interpreted this generosity as obligatory, but my mother's giving nature encompasses so much more than that at Sunday mass. She is always offering guests, friends, and neighbors food she had spent a great deal of time preparing or fancy treats she's picked up from her favorite specialty stores. And if she didn't have something to give, she always had a smile and a friendly pat on the shoulder or squeeze of the arm to make everyone feel welcome. It makes me smile when I do the same for others, knowing that it was my mother's influence that made me the way I am.

Taken together, although I appreciate but don't feel entirely aligned with stereotypical characteristics of American-Filipino families, the strong maternal characteristics deeply ingrained in Filipina culture are deeply ingrained in my life as well.

Spring: *Hospitality*

Catalina Lehrer

When asked by my Filipino mother to write a narrative on my memories of my exposure to and upbringing with Filipino culture, my first response was to give her a lighthearted hard time. She never taught me or my sisters her languages of Cebuano or

Cat and husband Jared visit Lola in Carcar, Cebu.

Tagalog, which I am forever sad about. I would have loved to be brought up bilingual.

When I questioned her as to why she never spoke her languages to me, she replied that my father was not Filipino nor fluent in Cebuano, so she did not have anyone at home to speak the language with. Although somewhat annoyed she did not teach me her native language, when thinking back there were certainly many subtle activities she did, possibly even subconsciously, that have made me a proud Filipina.

The most engrained and fond memories I have are the special-occasion, lumpia-making days. As most Filipinos know, making lumpia is a time and labor-intensive process. It involves cooking the stuffing, and most importantly gathering the family to help carefully wrap the lumpia. My dad was by far the best at stuffing the wraps, making a perfect fold, and brushing the egg yolks to glue it all together. The large spread of the food items to insert and the stack of lumpia wrappers were all lined up on the kitchen table like an assembly line. The house would smell for days after they were fried. I remember my friends in high school would come over on various occasions and be so excited to know lumpia was available as it was such a treat for them. In college, my then boyfriend, now husband, was put to work making lumpia when we would visit for holidays. As an adult, I asked my mom for the recipe and even purchased a small fryer to make our own. I had to search for a Filipino grocery store and make a half-hour drive for the specific Filipino lumpia wrappers required. These memories are such a gift, as I have many cherished hours of quality time spent with my family, especially my dad who is no longer with us.

Speaking of my dad, "they run on Filipino time" was a common phrase he would use in reference to my mom and her Filipino family, expecting them to be late. It was always a funny joke of the family and I thought it to be specific to my dad and his humor. As an adult, I became friends with a Filipino boy in college and while conversing about our families, he also mentioned "Filipino time." I laughed with him as he pointed out the phrase is common amongst many Filipinos, and not just a made-up line from my dad.

I had the pleasure of traveling to the Philippines ten years ago with my husband shortly after we were married. We spent time with my Filipino family, enjoyed lots and lots of lumpia, and experienced so many new cultural foods and experiences. We enjoyed many of my family's staples, including lechon, the garlic rice for breakfast, as well as the sumptuous buffets. We experienced Filipino kindness and humor, often bestowed upon my husband, as my family referred to him as "The Americano." My family made endless jokes over my husband's sweating due to the well-known heat and humidity.

Although I give my mom a hard time for not instilling her Filipino language upon me as a younger child, as I reminisce, there are many fond memories and experiences I have enjoyed throughout my life that involve my Filipino background and culture. As I look to pass these experiences on to my children, I am truly proud to be a Filipina, and I have my mom to thank for that.

Winter Afterthoughts

Upon reading what my three daughters have written, I felt an overwhelming gratitude and readiness for what lies ahead. There is so much to be thankful for because the paradigms shaping my life didn't lie wasted on the wayside. Instead, one way or another, they seeped through cultural and personal barriers.

Just as in the quadriptych painting, whole in itself but in panels that are detachable and able to be re-arranged, I am Mom of the Family in the winter of my life, merging with my daughters and their families like the never-ending rebirth of seasons, in varied colors, in rain and shine.

We know that even when children go away, we can still make connections, never allowing ideas, either ours or theirs, to get in the way. In this spirit, my three girls, Coco with the fall colors, Johanna with the summer ones, and Cat of the spring have shared their second-generation rediscoveries of Pinay values: living life simply, artistically, and orderly with diligence, restraint, compassion. And like the tiny seed of the Filipino almond tree called talisay, Filipino hospitality, practiced in even in the smallest ways, can be shared because generosity makes for togetherness.

Fe Baran lives in Pismo Beach, California, but remains united with friends in Hawai'i, who, although across the ocean, are so dearly held in her heart.

Seventeen

LIFE IS A DANCE

by Rosemarie Mendoza

I was born and raised in the Philippines. My dad was from Vigan while my mom was from Santa Cruz, Ilocos Sur, but I was born and raised in Manila. My mom travelled back and forth between Manila and the provinces. During summer, I would go to the Ilocos, Olongapo, and Baguio, where we had family.

My first language is Tagalog but I also speak Ilocano. When I used to go to the provinces, especially in Ilocos, my family, my relatives, my friends, all spoke Ilocano so I had to learn that language to be able to communicate with them.

I immigrated to Hawaii on April 15, 1974, close to 50 years ago—I was 15 then. My dad came here first in the early 1960s. He worked at Pearl Harbor as a plumber. My mom came in 1969, and my sister and I followed in 1974.

When my mom left the Philippines for Hawai'i, we were raised by my grandfather. My parents would send us money since my sister and I were still in school. When Martial Law came into effect, my mom was really afraid that we would be prevented from leaving the Philippines, so she started the paperwork to get us here.

When we left the Philippines, I was already enrolled at Far Eastern University. When I arrived in Hawai'i, I thought I would be placed in high school, but I was enrolled at Kalakaua Intermediate. In the Philippines back then, elementary school was only up to sixth grade—no seventh and eighth grades. But it was pretty good. I really enjoyed Kalakaua Intermediate since that's where I found my Ilocano and Tagalog friends.

When I started school, instead of putting me in a regular English class, I was placed in ESL (English as a Second Language). The teacher said, "You are in this class because you're an immigrant. You need to take this class for you to be able to speak English." But, I thought to myself, I do speak English. I write English. I understand English. As a matter of fact, when I was in the Philippines, all my courses were in English, except for one class which was in Tagalog.

I talked to the teacher. I said, "Well, I'm sorry, Mrs. Jacob, I think I'm in the wrong class." And she said, "What do you mean, you're in the wrong class?" I told her, "I am not an ABC person. I know how to speak English. I know how to write English. I don't think I belong in this class."

Mrs. Jacobs said, "Well, I don't know why you were placed here. I think you need to go and see the principal and the counselor and let them know."

That's exactly what I did. I went to the to the counselor's office. I said, "I think I'm in a wrong class, I need to go to a different class." The counselor said, "Well, you have to prove yourself. We'll make you an interpreter."

Kalakaua Intermediate had a lot of immigrants back then, especially Filipinos. When a student is asked to go to the principal's or counselor's office, either you're in trouble, or you have a question from the counselor. During these interactions, a translator is required so both the student and counselor could understand each other.

This is how I became a translator. The good thing about that role is that I could escape boring classes. I would be in my science or whatever class when suddenly, I would see someone coming in with a piece of yellow paper. The teacher would say, "Oh, Rosemarie, you're being called to the counselors' office."

All my classmates would look at me, like "you're in trouble again!" They didn't know that I was called to serve as translator.

It felt good doing that because I was helping my fellow Filipinos to be understood. They couldn't really express themselves. Now that I look back, it paved the way for my career as a human-resources professional in the travel and hospitality industries where housekeepers and other workers are Filipino. And I didn't realize that back then, one of the things that impressed my HR director was that I could speak both languages. It feels like a full circle to me—being placed at an ESL class at Kalakaua to my chosen career.

I also serve as interpreter in court cases, which is very, very difficult especially in arbitration cases. You need to use the right voice including the tone. You want to make sure that you're translating it in a way that fits the essence of the question.

I also understand a little bit of Bisaya, but since I don't practice the language, I lost some of the ability to speak it well. But when I speak to some of my Visayan friends, I can pick up what they're talking about.

When I was in the Philippines, I did folk dancing. When I came to Hawai'i, I looked for activities that would perpetuate my culture. I found friends at Kalakaua who were with the Filipiniana Dance Company that was directed by Aurelia Viernes. They asked me to join, and of course, I did readily. That's when I formed true friendships with a lot of people that I have kept until today.

While at Kalakaua, I was able to prove that I was fluent in speaking English and capable of doing high school work. So at the second half of the school year, I was transferred to Farrington High School. Just like most high school kids, I used to work part time after school. I would turn over my entire paycheck from Diners Drive-in to my mom, and she would give me money to spend. I wanted to keep all the money that I earned, but my mom said she was saving it for us.

While at Farrington, I became the president of the new Filipino Club. Our adviser back then was Mrs. Ethel Ward. I've always called her Mrs. Ward—she wants me to call her "Tita Ethel," but I said, "I'm sorry, Mrs. Ward--that's how I knew you. I respect you so much that I will keep on calling you Mrs. Ward."

Then: Rose and Troy Mendoza dancing Tinikling in 1982. Now: Teaching Zumba.

Back then during May Day at Farrington, the students danced the hula and honored the Hawaiian alii, or the queen and king and their court. I told Mrs. Ward, "Why can't we have Filipino folk dancing?" And she said, "That's a great idea! Why don't you tell the committee to do that?" And that's what we did—introduced Filipino folk dancing during May Day at a Hawai'i school.

That first year, we did the Tinikling. One of my good friends danced the Pandanggo sa Ilaw and we eventually added the dance with the banga (jar). It was then that I truly understood that I could promote Filipino culture by doing what I enjoyed best—folk dancing and speaking our languages well.

155

Most of us in the Filipino Club were immigrant teen-agers, first timers in Hawai'i. We wanted to travel to the other islands but needed funds to make it happen. Gems, one of the big department stores back then, was looking for folks to do their Christmas gift wrapping. That became one of our fundraising activities. We had different shifts so that all members of the club were able to participate. Our members showed a lot of initiative by asking customers, "Why don't we wrap your gifts for you?" It was so much fun; it added a feeling of 'ohana or sense of family.

We did so well that this fundraiser covered all our travel expenses. On Maui, we met another Filipino dance troupe. We entertained the residents of Molokai and travelled to the Big Island. Through these exchanges, we made life-long friends.

We had to perform in different places, so as a 16-year-old I had to get a driver's license. My parents didn't drive but used public transportation—The Bus. They had never driven in their lives, so I became the designated driver. This is how I learned to be very independent. I drove around Oahu.

We performed in libraries as part of the Filipino Club, the Filipiniana Dance Company, or Operation Manong, a program where older Filipino college students mentored the younger ones still in high school. We danced at conventions and family parties. After school, about ten of us would travel all the way to Haleiwa or to Turtle Bay on Oahu's North Shore. We would perform until 10 o'clock at night, and then return to Honolulu. We not only presented Filipino dances but also added a bit of Spanish and some hula. We showcased the diverse cultures of Hawai'i—something that I don't see anymore. It was through dance that I learned to appreciate the various cultures of Hawai'i.

Interestingly, the dance instructors and directors were all different, not just in their personalities and behaviors, but their approaches to discipline and teaching. Some were strict; some just wanted you to learn the dance routine. Some were very professional because when you perform in public, you are representing your country, the Philippines. Everything had to be uniform and consistent. I danced with the various companies. The Pearl of the Orient (under Pat Valentin of the Big Island) used to perform at the Royal Hawaiian Hotel and some of its lead dancers eventually formed their own dance troupes. H. Wayne Mendoza taught dance at the University of Hawai'i with his group, Himigbayan, where I was also a member. George Ragasa formed the Manileña and had a big showroom at the Chinese Cultural Center. I had the privilege to dance with the "Sydette Show" under George Ragasa and Zack Labez. One of the girls who used to be with Filipiniana formed her own troupe on Maui. She not only taught dance but also sewed costumes and included Hawaiian hula in her repertoire.

When you're on stage, you develop self-confidence, especially when you are dancing in front of thousands of people. It is through dance that I met many life-long friends such as Alfredo Evangelista, Sonia Lugmao Aranza, and Vicky Ramil (who danced with Pamana and who also was my manang at Operation Manong). It is also through dance that I met my husband—one of the three Mendoza brothers in the Filipiniana Dance Company.

Dancing is a wonderful way to perpetuate a culture. It is unfortunate that those golden days of Filipino folk dancing in the islands are gone. There are a few groups here and there, but not with the same popularity as before.

Those were memorable days. I have retained my fluency in the Filipino languages of Tagalog and Ilocano which helped me immensely in my career and business initiatives. My husband and I have translated our love for Filipino folk dancing into teaching Zumba, using popular Filipino contemporary songs to encourage folks to maintain healthy lifestyles.

Dance and language are my choices in preserving the culture of my homeland.

Rosemarie Mendoza *retired from her human resources career and is now president of Nature's Atmospheric Water Systems powered by AKVO, an air-to-water technology that creates both water and clean air. She and her husband Troy have been married for more than 30 years. They have a son and two beautiful granddaughters.*

Eighteen

QUERIDA, MADRASTA, INA

by Divina Telan-Robillard

"So?" was his reply. I think I blinked twice quickly in disbelief.

One word. He said one word, not two. It wasn't even the word I expected, nor was the emotion that I sensed came with it. I expected disgust. Instead, did I perceive less of a judgement than merely a need for further clarification? The feeling of relief seeped in much, much later that night in the cover of darkness in my bedroom, when things got clearer in my mind and spirit. I was keenly and thankfully aware of redemption, no longer self-retribution.

We were sitting on one of the low lava rock walls that terraced the hotel's garden. Sokeh's rock, the iconic natural stone formation of Ponape (now Pohnpei, in post-Compact of Free Association with the United States), loomed in the distant across the bay, illuminated by a gorgeous early spring moon. The air was heavy with water that threatened to become a downpour later that night. Professor Britt Robillard was in the same plane to Ponape as I. From the moment we exchanged looks in the airplane, he had been aggressively pursuing every opportunity to talk, whether in the hospital where we both worked with different teams, to dinner in the restaurant in the hotel we just happened to be staying together. Initially, I was amused/flattered by his actions, but this evening's talk after dinner was more serious. He talked about following me to Manila.

I knew I had to divulge my secret life, the earlier the better to avoid unnecessary complications. Thus, to see how sincere he was, I had just bluntly confessed that I was somebody's mistress.

I was confused by his response. He couldn't have known that with one word, a myth that had been accepted as gospel truth through generations in my conservative Filipino multiverse was being shattered. His one word, uttered in complete innocence, zapped away the subliminal ache under the even-keel façade with which I normally face the world. Unable to break free from an errant relationship, I had been in a raging battle within, endlessly questioning my own morals and upbringing, simultaneously suffering the pain of guilt, shame, and anger after each tryst and stupidly longing for the next.

I had been in an affair with a married man for a year. I wasn't forced into it; I had freely yielded to my forbidden feelings, given my combustible combination of impatience, loneliness, and rebellion against prevailing unfair gender double standards. My lover's declaration that he was never leaving his wife and family kept me constantly reviewing my actions. I was at the point of realizing I was not equipped to thrive in a "life in sin."

The past year, I led a double life: an open one of an accomplished professional whose educational pedigree and achievements were held in high esteem, and a darker, secret one of clandestine out-of-town trysts and furtive calls. With the constant angst of being discovered whilst traipsing in the verboten, the future looked bleak. The insecure life of a querida would ensure that the longed-for ideal of motherhood would totally be out of the question; I would never bring forth illegitimate children. Even when/if, in time, the life of a pamilya sa ikalawang asawa/anak sa querida (family with a second wife/child with a mistress) were to find tolerated acceptance in our urban ghetto neighborhood, the gossip and sneers would never stop.

Aling Gelay: Pssst, Pacing. Tignan mo yung nasa kantong naka-saya ng berde.
(Look at that lady in the corner with the green skirt.)
Points with pursed lips.

Aling Pacing: Sino, yung si Dibina? Yung panganay nina Alma?
(You mean, Divina? Alma's older sister?)

Aling Gelay: Oo, halika. May balita ako tungkol diyan.
(Yes, come. I have news about her.)

Aling Gelay: Makinig ka: eto ang drama. Mukhang may asawa si lalaki!
(Listen. Here's the rub. It appears the man is married!)

Aling Pacing: Siyanga? Diyan na ako di maniniwala sa iyo. Paano naman nalaman, aber?
(Really? That's hard to believe. How did you know that?)

Aling Gelay: Aba eh, may wedding ring sa daliri! Medyo may edad pa raw, kulot ang buhok, at may bigote!!!!
(He had a wedding ring on his finger! He is somewhat older, curly-haired, and mustachioed!)

Aling Pacing: Ay, kawawang Aling Lourdes. Siya pa naman ang inaasahan nilang makakatulong sa pagtatapos ng mga kapatid, ano? Sayang lang ang dunong. Tsk, tsk.
(Poor Aling Lourdes! They had banked on her helping their family with the younger children's schooling, yeah? Pity that she's so smart! Tsk, tsk.)

My private life as the subject of malicious gossip at the corner store and neighborhood wakes was not something I had imagined for myself. I am sure my parents dreamt of only the most desirable paths for me. In general, our society organizes a set of "expectations" for bringing up children and rearing them to be outstanding citizens. The consequence of tacking close to

161

these expectations is reward (approval, openness, acceptance) and for deviance, punishment (ostracism, censure, disapproval). To help their girls grow along the proper paths, Filipino parents need only mention these expectations, inserted into conversations during teachable moments. In time, these expectations are internalized, becoming the template upon which the girl would pattern her life and define her life choices.

Take for instance the expectation that a girl should remain sexually innocent until the matrimonial bed, or as "damaged goods" risk having a bad reputation never to be seriously considered altar material. A socially aware girl needs to constantly watch out for situations that could lead to sexual dalliance, to "always keep her legs firmly together" and not give in to a young man's persuasions no matter how alluring. As Mama would say, every young man just wants to get into your pants, and once he has achieved his goal, you would no longer be desired by him or taken seriously by other men. Following Mama's logic, the impure girl loses currency and becomes easy prey for men who just want a good time, fair game to acquire as a querida, a woman of loose morals.

For us women who achieved puberty in the 1970s, we were also reminded to pay attention to the ticking of our biological clocks. This had been my experience when, unmarried past age 25, I had yet to enlist a single serious suitor. Being dark skinned, short, flat-nosed AND poor, I was not exactly the woman that young Filipinos of my generation would consider a dream catch.

So when Dr. Britt Robillard, with his one word, unknowingly raised my status from damaged goods to good-as-new, we embarked on a courtship that sizzled through the post. When he arrived in Manila that summer, I rewarded him with my matamis na "oo" (my sweet "yes") but not until after I bailed out of my shady relationship with Lover via a surreptitiously short (and light) mourning period. I am very certain I positively glowed in my resurrected status as wanted/desired, once again beguiling.

162

A church wedding at the Philippine Independent Church of the Infant Jesus in Manila was held to acquiesce to Divina's family, who was not too happy with just a civil wedding.

Never mind that Britt was only now furiously working on his stalled divorce (at that time, separated from his wife with whom he shared a couple of young children)! Like Scarlett O'Hara, I told myself I would deal with these issues—divorce situation, stepchildren—in due time.

But then again, my mother had misgivings about me moving to Honolulu.

"Masyadong malayo, anak! Wala kang kamag-anak doon! Paano na lang kung magkasakit ka? (It's too far, child! You don't have any relatives there. How would it be if you were to get sick)" she worriedly intoned one afternoon a few days before the quiet civil wedding we had planned for August.

I was grading some papers on the kitchen table while Mama was winnowing rice, the rhythmic up and down movement of her bilao (basket) unbroken until, tilting it right and left, she blew off the chaff onto a sack laid flat on the cement floor.

"Aysus, Mama! First world ang U.S., di ba? Number one sa health care," I said, looking up from my work, trying on a jesting tone to lighten the mood. "Siguro naman, makakahanap ako ng mga kapwang Pinay nurse sa ospital, noh (I am almost sure I could find a Pinay nurse in the hospital, right)?"

"Aba, eh, kung magsusuplada ka doon tulad nang gawi mo dito, lalasunin ka nila, kahit kapwa mo Piilipino (Well, if you continue being such a snob, they will surely poison you)!"

She persisted, "Lalo na't may mga anak sa unang asawa! Akala mo ba madaling maging madrasta (Especially since the first wife has children. Do you think it is easy to be a stepmother)?"

High on love and the excitement of the upcoming wedding, not even my mother's cautioning words could dampen my spirits. Nevertheless, they proved to be prophetic.

We got married in the summer of 1982. After I turned in the grades at the end of the fall semester, I flew to Honolulu as

Britt's wife. Having redeemed myself by getting respectably married, I thought I would be rid of the cultural demons that had caused me so much anguish in my dark, recent past.

I was spectacularly wrong. Migration only moved my physical self from Motherland and Mother. Mama never let me forget that I was Britt's pangalawang asawa (second wife). Ex-wife was always either asawa (wife) or unang asawa (first wife). The first reference irritated me no end, and the second—a reminder that I was NOT the first—irritated me even more! Since my mother was the most dominant force in my life, the stereotype continued to haunt me, and thus, to hurt. In other words, I may have left the Philippines, but the Philippines never left me.

There being no formal marital status as divorce in the Philippines of my time, there simply was no model in the Pinoy psyche for the configuration of second marriage. Lacking the proper vocabulary, society employed terms such as pangalawang asawa/pamilya (second wife/family). The problem was this carried negative connotations.

There exist many families from relationships with a querida or kinakasama (common-law relationship). It is well known that Philippine society exhibits what Fr. James Bulatao, S.J. in his writings referred to as "split-level Catholicism:" the "coexistence within the same person of two or more thought-and-behavior systems which are inconsistent with each other." Thus, the many querida/kinakasama (mistress/common law) families in the only Catholic nation in Asia.

The existential cultural void vis-à-vis divorce also affected my relationship with Britt's children. In the early years of our marriage, I was often bewildered by my lack of warmth toward the kids and a civil but cold stance in the very few times Ex-wife and I shared the same breathing space. The divorce, being far from amicable, could easily explain the latter, but the children?

Hope Sabanpan-Yu, in describing the treatment of stepmothers in three Cebuano novels, points to the commonly accepted definition of "family" as a natural group of people related by blood. It becomes problematic when an unrelated woman—the stepmother or madrasta—enters the picture. In the Philippines of my era, the only accepted stepfamily relationship is a remarriage following the death of a spouse. Disney and Brothers Grimm fairy tales reinforced the notion of the wicked stepmother. Thus, deservedly or not, the stepmother role carries with it a negative charge.

Consciously or not, I complicated life further by continuing to apply the querida model to my divorce/family situation. In a Venn diagram, this was how I perceived our relationship to be.

Ex-wife Kids BRITT Me

One evening, a year into our marriage, the stressful situation came to a head. The kids and I, having just finished our showers and preparing for bed, were in the bedroom of our apartment. We had spent the whole day at the beach and all of us were tired. Britt went out to pick up dinner. I was seating on the floor combing Girl's long tresses, while trying to ignore Boy who was on our bed and whining, threatening to escalate into one of his wild tantrums. All of a sudden, Boy sent a hairbrush flying through the air, missing my head by inches. That's when I lost it. In a frightful rage, I flew off the floor onto the bed, and tightly held his now-trembling arms against his side.

In my most Wicked Stepmother voice, I managed to say, "You. Do. Not. Throw. Anything. At. Me. Understand?" I could see fear in Boy's eyes, but in seconds, mine misted over with burning hot tears. I flew out the front door after slamming it behind me, into the darkly quiet Honolulu streets.

I don't remember how long I walked; I knew I wanted to go somewhere to decompress. A few blocks away, I saw a cross above a building I surmised was a church. I walked by the mock orange hedges lining the now closed side entrances. I dropped onto the cement floor and leaned against the corner of a wall, far from the front entrance. I stayed there for a while, crying my heart out: homesick, lonely, not yet settled into my new roles and relationships, the different culture, and speaking English all the time.

Calmed down, probably a good couple hours later, I walked back to our building, where I found Britt pacing frantically, the kids quiet in a corner. They had just driven back home after looking for me all over the area near the Philippine Consulate! During our talk that evening, Britt and I teased out the source of my concerns. When I showed him my Venn diagram, he drew, for me, this version of our relationship.

Once again, my imperturbable partner played clarifier-of-ill-applied-culturally-transmitted conceptions.

When Britt was diagnosed with ALS (Amyotrophic Lateral Sclerosis or Lou Gehrig's Disease) in the second year of our marriage, the difficulties worsened. We were all overwhelmed by the tentacles of chronic, debilitating, image-destroying, confidence-busting, unpredictable trajectory of ALS. Living with a fatal diagnosis had its own particular dynamic that, for me, brought immense emotional and spiritual growth while rendering constant stress to the psyche and body.

In 1987, life changed when we had Son. It was a pregnancy that Britt and I both wanted. I would have a family of my own complete with a father that won't come and go; a father who would openly acknowledge us as his, never mind that he was disabled all of Son's life. It made being a madrasta a lot less quizzical, perhaps because through Son, I had a smidgen of biological connection to my stepchildren. Motherhood diffused whatever stepfamily concerns we were having.

With Son's birth, I became an ina (mother) through the socially acceptable route to motherhood: marriage first. When Son was five, our adopted Daughter arrived from the Philippines. She is my younger sister's daughter and my goddaughter in baptism; that makes me her ninang (godmother).

It is now almost seven years after Britt died, having lived with ALS for a remarkable 31 years. I am 68 years old. I had been a querida, a madrasta, and ina. Among all the roles I have played. being a querida was the toughest. Only a few of my closest friends know, and then, only recently. It was neither easy to live or talk about it. But I figured, at this age, very few would get hurt if it were brought to the open. After all, the people who would have cared most are now dead; and those living would probably not care too much.

At the third act of life, I look back at how I lived and understand how my experiences contributed to my world view and growth. By sharing it openly, I hope it can shed light on the social myths/mysteries young women may encounter and the repercussions that may happen whether these situations occur within or beyond the borders of the Motherland.

Divina Telan-Robillard lives in Kailua on Oahu, Hawai'i with her daughter and her retired soldier-husband, and two grandkids. She has few regrets in life, one of which is not resigning fully from her teaching job to raise her son alongside caregiving for her husband. Instead, it was her parents who took care of Son in his early life. Her stepchildren live in San Francisco and in Kailua.

Nineteen

BABAYLAN MULI*

by Katherine Baltazar

Entering the 21st century as a woman of Filipino-Swiss roots, I began to get curious during the Crone's phase of my life (which one enters in menopause) as to which parts of my lineages I trace my heritage as a healer. It would seem an obvious answer as two of my Filipino aunts were nurses and one a dietician.

But because my first language was Swiss-German Gothic, a vestige of German, in my early years I tended to gravitate more to my maternal side. I spoke Swiss-German until I started kindergarten. On my mother's side, there were mostly landowners, farmers, judges, and men who served as mercenaries in foreign militaries. The most famous was an ancestor who fought in Napoleon Bonaparte's army and received a medal of appreciation when he left. In my own immediate family, my Filipino father and his two brothers were part of the U.S. Air Force, Army, and Navy.

My mother met my father at a Sunday high tea gathering at the International Student House in Washington DC. My father was an Air Force lieutenant who, because of his aptitude for languages, was sent at the height of the Cold War to study Russian at Georgetown University. After working as a governess in Paris (young Swiss women at the time had a reputation for being good governesses) where she learned French, my mother

*Babaylan Again

169

wanted to acquire another language, English. Finding a Jewish family in Washington, DC, she crossed the Atlantic, as many people did in those days, by boarding a boat in London for the three-and-a-half-day crossing.

It wasn't until I was six years old that we came to live in the Philippines where we met my father's mother, Isabel, our lola, though we called her Grandma. She and my Grandpa Pedro, a chemist who worked for the Meralco Electric Company, lived on Kanlaon Street in Quezon City. The house was bought for them by their eldest daughter, who we called Tante (German term for aunt) Lulu. She completed her nurses training at the University of Santo Tomas, and with my father's help, came by boat to the U.S. where she acquired her master's degree from Loyola University in Chicago. She never married but remained a faithful nurse working at hospitals in Chicago and at St. Luke's Hospital in New York City for 25 years. Her two younger sisters also entered the medical field. Tante Julie got her master's degree at Catholic University and Tante Lety, became a dietician, working at Cornell Hospital, where she met and married a cardiologist.

Following the paternal lineage, my sister and I both became nurses. My sister skipped a year in high school as she intended to go into pre-med, but then after a semester at Iowa State University, changed her mind and went into nursing. I originally had wanted to be an Egyptologist, then an oceanographer and a veterinarian.

One of my childhood heroes was Albert Schweitzer, who started a hospital in Lambaréné in French Equatorial Africa (Gabon). He won the 1952 Nobel Peace Prize for his principle of "reverence for life," driven by the religious and ethical imperatives to help others. I entered Marymount College to study political science but when Watergate broke in 1975, I switched to nursing.

By age 47 and still single, my nursing career eventually would attract me to Medical Mission Sisters, whose charism is "to be a healing presence in a wounded world." I entered in 2002 and remained a religious sister for 19 years. My best years was being in mission on the Cheyenne River Sioux Reservation in South Dakota from 2012 to 2017, working for the tribe as a psychiatric nurse practitioner.

I wondered what had drawn me to Native Peoples. One strong affinity was to their earth-based spirituality. Over time, I came to recognize yet another dimension, a racial aspect that I had not fully dealt with. When I lived in the Philippines, I could see that my father had an elevated status in the eyes of his kababayan (countrymen) because he had a white wife.

A distinct memory stands out. At age six, in those early months after our arrival, my grandmother wanted to take my sister and me to visit one of her friends. We had put on our dresses upstairs and came downstairs to show my mother that grandma had powdered our faces. My mother chuckled and then directed us to go back upstairs and take it off, but my grandmother said no; she needed to show we had a white mother.

As time went on, I observed how people responded differently to my mother simply because of her whiteness. I found there was something wrong with this; it was not based on merit of her character, but on her skin color. I frequently would hear the sing-song acclamation, "Ah, mestiza!" (always said with a raised voice inflection at the end). I would have been too young to understand the effects of colonialism at that age. In the early 1960s in Switzerland, all of us five little brown-skinned children and our tall, darker-skinned father were perhaps the darkest that some people had ever seen in my grandmother's town. My brothers would get angry when they would be called kleine Negerlein—little negros—by the village boys. I don't recall being called one, but because I knew it wasn't so, it never bothered me like it did my brothers.

On the Lakota reservation, it was the opposite—mixed blood was looked as lesser than full bloods. Close family connections are similar in the Lakota and Filipino cultures. In traditional families, children are called according to their role in the family—older brother or younger sister. In Tagalog, older brother is kuya and older sister is ate. And like Filipinos, the Lakota are a deeply prayerful people. Prayers were always being offered for healing. Although it's been 400 years since they have been colonized by Christian missionaries, some no longer pray to a Christian God but to Wakan Tanka, Great Spirit. When in 1978 President Nixon signed the American Indian Religious Freedom Act (AIRFA) granting the freedom to practice Native religions, many returned to their original spirituality.

I attended several ceremonies, pow wows, and sweats in my time on the prairie. There is much preparation for the Lakota's Sundance. During Sundance season, the staff would empty out to attend. In recent years, women have also started to pierce their flesh, confining it to their upper forearms and not the upper pectoral region as with the men. When my brother came to visit with his family one summer, he was honored at the Sundance by being called to share the pipe with the drum group (because his skin color made them think he was Native?). The Sundance can be seen to be deeply intertwined with the passion story as was acknowledged by Jesuit Fr. William Stolzman in his 1986 book, "The Pipe and Christ." It was always heartbreaking for me to see how the early missionaries could not recognize the deep spirituality of the people.

Because the veil is so thin between the secular and the spiritual, I could often ask if patients had been visited by their deceased family members in dreams. Most times, the answer was yes, and because I could have longer appointments at the Indian Health Service, we would frequently include spiritual matters in our sessions.

I had always been drawn to nature-based spirituality and indigenous medicines. When I moved to Zurich, Switzerland in my twenties to attend the CG Jung Institute, Europe was having a resurgence (wiederkehr) of Celtic lore. I latched on to that current and embarked on connecting with Celtic spirituality that ran through my mother's linage. The town she was born in bears a Celtic name—Wohlhusen; wohl meaning good, well, comfortable; cozy; husen indicating a manor on which tenants tilled the land and raised livestock in turn for protection from the lord of the manor. These Celtic farming communities would have included a Druid priest who determined the proper preparation of seeds, read the stars to determine when planting season was to start, and performed rituals that began any planting or harvesting event.

Katherine and a Native American friend at the reservation.

In my thirties, I spent time among the curanderos (healers) in Oaxaca, Mexico, went to live in the foothills of the Himalayas to study Tibetan medicine, pursued Maori medicine while visiting New Zealand, and lived on an aboriginal reserve in the New Territory in Australia. During my five years in Hawai'i, I was in the class of the revered Hawaiian herbalist Papa Auwai, who taught Hawaiian medicine. At one point, I tried to synthesize all this into an academic study, but somehow, that window never opened.

As I took stock of all this exposure to indigenous medicines and practices, I realized there was nothing indigenous that I could call my own. With the sensitivity growing around "appropriation" of cultures, I began to look for what I could claim from my own heritage, something I would not have to appropriate. It was only around 2020 that I began delving into my Filipino healing roots.

It was an email from Dr. Ruth Mabanglo to the Filipino Association of University Women (FAUW) where I first heard the word babaylan, a Visayan name for Filipinos who function as healers, shamans, seers, and community "miracle-workers." What surprised me was that most of the babaylan were female.

My readings introduced me to Leny Mendoza Strobel and the Babaylan Studies. In her material, I recognized I had come to a source that would lead me back into a tradition that I had never been exposed. Leny Mendoza Strobel writes about her own journey, "And so this has been the draw to begin more fully embracing the animist world view that was prevalent as their world view—where the world is alive and animated. This was a world view that encompassed seven realms—the underground, the earth, the oceans, the sky, the spirit realm of our anitos and ancestors, the planetary realm, and the cosmos; nothing new in how we conceive of the world, except that the babaylan…were able to receive communications from it to them and they to them." They had access to these realms that I had read about, a familiar cosmology of many of the indigenous cultures with whom I had lived and studied. I was beginning to recognize a new direction in wishing to experience this myself.

New places and unfamiliar cultures have always held an attraction for me, but not necessarily in the ancestral realms. Was my Cronehood finally making me wise enough to hear the ancestors calling me? Appropriation aside, could this also be a resurgence of the babaylan, given the state of our world? Could I be responding to their ancient call (or has it always been responded to, since there are so many Filipino nurses in the world)?

My father had shared that his maternal grandmother would have the neighbors come to her for spiritual guidance. He described that she had one of those old-fashioned iron keys on a cord loosely tied around her bible. The person would ask a question and then watch the key turn in one direction for a yes, and another for a no. I imagined him and his siblings secretly looking in onto the scene where only the adults were gathered.

My Tante Lulu was born breech. Apparently, there is a superstition that breech people are given special powers to guide chicken or fish bones caught in someone's throat by stroking the throat to bring the bone down the esophagus. When I asked her about this, she said it worked.

So, what does all this say about my inherited abilities? Not much. I am neither psychic nor have magnetic hands. Yet, I see us at the cusp of paradigm shifts that are calling for the babaylan to return in the modern context.

I currently work with ketamine therapy, a form of psychedelic therapy with tremendous potential to expand consciousness and allow people to step out of their everyday personal, ego-centric consciousness to experience a more global, universal consciousness. Ketamine is approved treatment for major depressive and anxiety disorders such as OCD, PTSD, and Bipolar II. Psychedelics are revolutionizing psychiatry, as they are also being studied for treatment of substance abuse and eating disorders. I have witnessed the healing that has occurred after six weeks of ketamine treatment and have undergone seven sessions where I have experienced cosmic scenes. Developed in 1962 as a fast-acting anesthetic, ketamine was later discovered to increase synaptic connections between neurons in the brain, as well as release BDNF (Brain Derived Neurotropic Factor), a molecule involved in plastic learning and memory. In this work, my colleagues and I help those who have not been helped by conventional treatments.

In this time of massive global and political change, people turn to healers looking to restore the imbalances that are disrupting their lives. This is the time mother earth is drawing our attention to healing. Healers are being called upon, as of old, to help rebalance the body/mind and to restore the reverence for life so that we might continue to thrive on this precious planet. We are each being called to first heal ourselves before we heal humankind and restore respect towards the planet that sustains us.

Katherine Baltazar is of Filipino-Swiss heritage. Her first language was Swiss German. Her father, a Russian linguist, was the first Filipino-born officer in the Air Force. As part of a military family, she lived seven years of her childhood in the Philippines and other parts of the world. In her adult life, she continues to travel and pursue an interest in indigenous healing practices. In recent years, she has been making the connection to the ancestral roots that lead her to the healing profession.

Twenty

SCHOLAR WARRIOR OF KAPU ALOHA AND MAHALAYA

by Alma M. Ouanesisouk Trinidad

I live in the diaspora. The motherland of Paoay, Ilocos Norte, Philippines is the home of my parents and grandparents who settled in Hawai'i by means of the sugar and pineapple industries. Both maternal and paternal grandfathers were sakada. I met Grandpa Leodigario (my dad's dad) when I was just an infant; he worked in a plantation on Maui, and then Moloka'i. Grandpa Tomas (my mom's dad) worked on a plantation in Hilo, Big Island.

I was born on the island of Moloka'i. I have fond memories of communal life and closeness. It's interesting that I refer to this time of my life—birth till 13 years—as profound and key to the formation of cultural values related to community and love for the land. As a Filipino, growing up on Moloka'i provided the first lessons in appreciating humble beginnings, sharing of resources such as food (e.g., vegetables grown in a family garden, fish, chicken, pig, deer) and money (e.g., mutual aid when someone passed away; a group loan to purchase something). That seems to have been lost when my family was displaced when the pineapple plantation company, Del Monte, shut down in the late 1980s. We moved to Kunia on Oahu. Two generations of my family worked in the pineapple plantations. I was devastated. I mourn that loss, even to this day.

My childhood living on Moloka'i and adolescence years going to Mililani High School were essential to my earlier understanding of oppression, power, and privilege. It was during this time I faced deep internalized oppression. I was ashamed and embarrassed of being Filipina. I heard a lot of stereotypes about our people: can't speak good English; eat "black dog;" Filipina girls are "easy" or "sluts;" Filipino guys are "gangsters," smoke too much "batu," and always make trouble. I was also ashamed to be from Kunia, a former pineapple plantation village. I often felt that we were poor because we didn't have a big house like my friends who lived in Mililani and my parents worked for a pineapple company, while my friends' parents were highly educated. I also was surrounded by mixed Filipinos who denied their Filipino background.

My stomping grounds of college at University of Hawai'i at Manoa (UHM) continued to be a venue for understanding disparities and gaps in education. Here, I learned about the high rates of high school dropouts and the lack of clear pathways to higher education, and mental health issues such as substance abuse, youth suicide, violence, and illnesses like diabetes among Filipino and Asian Pacific Islander communities. I began to learn the different life experiences based on Indigenous, refugees, and immigrant statuses. The human struggles that stem from these disparities and gaps piqued my curiosity of what it means for our communities to overcome oppressive conditions.

Upon graduation from UHM, I left Hawai'i for graduate school at the University of Michigan, Ann Arbor. I thought that leaving the island would provide me with the opportunity to explore new places and people. And yes, it did! The one year being away provided me with diverse exposure to the human experiences of struggle, this time of African American, Latino, and Hmong communities. It took being away from Hawai'i and being connected and mentored by scholars of color to deepen my consciousness of oppression and exploitation faced by minority communities of color.

Upon earning my Master's in Social Work, I returned to Moloka'i in 1999 to work for Moloka'i Community Services Council. The island had received a huge federal grant to revitalize and redevelop the community in multiple ways—education, health, economy, land, and more. My nearly two years working on my home island provided me with tangible insights into what freedom could be achieved through social development, coordination, and implementation of culturally responsive and Native Hawaiian value-centered programs. The programs engaged the community with a process from design to implementation.

After that, I spent several more years working for the State of Hawai'i Department of Health as part of research teams exploring mental health disparities among youth and families, and with the Kamehameha Schools' research and policy analysis and systems evaluation team.

Then I embarked on a voyage of earning a PhD in social welfare. I had become frustrated by the disparities and gaps in education and health among Native Hawaiians, Filipinos, and other communities. I saw the need for research to be developed, designed, and implemented by, for, and with community. I also had growing concerns about policies that were implemented that did not consider culture and history. I needed to channel these feelings to something more tangible and useful. I knew, or at least from what I had observed, that one equipped with a doctorate degree tended to be invited to the table. I applied to two doctoral degree programs, was accepted by both, and chose the University of Washington (UW) in Seattle.

At UW, I was part of the first doctoral cohort of diverse backgrounds—more than 75 percent self-identified as coming from communities of color. It was a monumental milestone for the school. But while I had the opportunity to address my community concerns, I also began to realize how much of my schooling and professionalization had been "whitewashed"— meaning framing minority characteristics as deficits and not strengths, based on the majority culture's standards of success. I also observed how policies, even those that led to programs and services for our communities, could sometimes limit change and healing. Although I felt sadness, these realizations brought me to a place of yearning to rediscover my Filipino roots and values.

I had taken Ilocano language courses at UH Manoa and was heavily involved in Filipino-centric extracurricular activities, including the Sariling Gawa Youth Council, where I served as youth delegate, then became its board president. In Seattle, I immersed myself in the local Filipino community, learning about its history and issues. I started networking with other Filipino scholars. The doctoral degree provided me with a ticket to work on pan-Asian-Pacific-Islander (API) issues in the Pacific Northwest.

In 2009, as a PhD candidate/ABD (all but dissertation), I started working at Portland State University (PSU), School of Social Work (SSW). I was the first to be appointed to a shared position with the SSW, Child and Family Studies, and University Studies' undergraduate general education program. I became PSU's first Filipina-tenured professor, joining the handful of tenured API professors.

In the next six years, I focused on building relationships among API and other communities of color. As a scholar, I see my role, no matter if I am a researcher, instructor, or volunteer, as a facilitator of inclusion, equity, and social change. Knowledge production is a shared process, one that is a dance of collaboration and partnership. Because of this work, I was recognized as one of eight finalists of the 2015 Ernest A. Lynton Award for Scholarship of Engagement for Early Career Faculty. This award honors scholars who connect teaching, research/creative activity, and service to community engagement in the context of social justice. Although I did not win the award, it was remarkable to be a finalist among a pool of 42 extraordinary candidates from a variety of universities and disciplines.

The Trinidad-Ouanesisouks (l to r): Honorio Kainoa, Alma, Hongkham, and Araya Lynn at the Foundation for Philippine Progress gala. Alma is the Foundation board chair.

I consider my achievements as an exercise in surviving among the weeds of toxic white supremacy. I say this, because my work in expanding and integrating API communities came with the lack of support and validation. With slim structural processes, one was faced with constant biases in pursuing research pertaining to API, let alone Filipino studies. Service on diversity, inclusion, and equity committees and initiatives did not seem to count towards tenure and promotion.

Nevertheless, I do want to highlight the fact that the relationships built among former students and the general community yielded growing momentum and critical mass that fueled a focus on Filipino issues.

PSU is still a predominantly white university. But in the last two years, I have seen a surge in the enrollment of Filipino and API students. I have witnessed growth—former students becoming colleagues and more entering an array of careers and professions. We now have another Pinay professor on the tenure track. This past summer was the first time I mentored a team of three McNair* undergraduate scholars who self-identify as Pinays/Filipina Americans. That is a huge, monumental milestone for me. Change is happening all around.

I want to take the time to reflect on how pressing forward for freedom and love for our community comes with both joy and exhaustion. I hope we can honor the tension. While serving on multiple search committees, courageous and contentious discussions took place. It helped that students were demanding to have more faculty members who reflect the diverse student population, as well as curricula that include their cultures and community needs. To secure a Pinay scholar's appointment required ongoing advocacy for not only diversity in recruitment of scholars, but equity in the hiring process.

To have more Pinays in research involved repetitive framing of the work to be seen as relevant to community needs, as well as motivators for student participation. Research can help liberate, heal, and elevate our communities, and serve as a tool to advance change. One has to articulate these needs multiple times to multiple people of power, often feeling disappointed that infrastructure and processes are not being put in place fast enough.

With that being said, I share two recent initiatives I am a part of: first, an Asian American and Pacific Islanders Studies Program; and second, an ad hoc committee on crafting language on diversity, equity, and inclusion for the University Promotion and Tenure guidelines. Being part of these two efforts, I feel the heavy lifting. I am fully aware that revolution(s) for our communities, must be done by the community, within individuals and families—decolonizing minds, empowering, healing, and liberating ourselves. Simultaneously, I find a glimmer of hope among my children and extended families in the diaspora.

My children are mixed Filipino, Lao, and Indian. They have witnessed my experience as a Pinay Scholar Warrior, as well as their father's career path in the tech field. During these multiple pandemics and crises, we are having deep discussions about what we are observing, witnessing, and experiencing. As a family unit, we aim to foster a sense of responsibility and accountability to become part of the change.

Right after earning tenure, I gifted myself the time to be part of a human rights mission to the Philippines. I had never been home to the motherland since I was an infant. My partner and I spent time visiting long-lost family members and paying tribute to my grandparents by visiting their graves in my barrio. The love for my Filipino family, ancestors, culture, and community grew.

The COVID crisis provided the opportunity to connect across oceans and lands. Thanks to technology, we were able to gather virtually to celebrate my parents' 52nd wedding anniversary, touch base with a sick elder, learn more about each other, and about the land from where our ancestors come. Unsettling discussion on land ownership among family, and the rediscovery of family stories emerged during this time. I am not sure if this would have been possible, but I am finding this hopeful for the near future.

I identify as a Pinay scholar warrior of kapu (sacred in Hawaiian), aloha (love in Hawaiian), and mahalaya (love and freedom; in Tagalog). I pause in amazement at the strength and survival of the communities I serve, come from, and stand in solidarity with. I grapple and attempt to make sense of the cultural values of love and freedom in the midst of ongoing threats to our wellbeing and livelihoods. I remember the contentious history of displacement, forced migration, and contemporary enslavements of our peoples. Being a descendant of the sakada and having affiliations with the Laos refugees' experience while witnessing my life partner's families and communities, I see historical and contemporary trauma permeate in our communities. I hope to demonstrate my vulnerabilities, so that I may identify and rediscover sources to heal and reground myself to my life's personal and professional purposes. I hope sharing my voice brings strength, hope, and inspiration from within and throughout. May we rise up from our shared, parallel experiences as Pinays.

The PSU McNair Scholars Program works with selected first-generation, low-income, and under-represented undergraduates who want to pursue PhDs. McNair scholars conduct research under the supervision of faculty mentors and create effective strategies for getting into and graduating from doctoral programs. (http://www.pdx.edu/mcnair-program/)

Alma Trinidad *is a full professor and the Bachelor of Social Work Program Director/Chair at Portland State University, School of Social Work. Her areas of scholarship, teaching, practice, and service include critical pedagogues of place, anti-oppressive and liberatory social work, social movements, and macro social work (e.g., organizations, policies, and community).*

Twenty One

MAHJONG!
Double Dice

by Nanette Carreon-Ruhter

Chow!

Pong!

Secret!

Laoshi, you have not given me a chow yet.

Oh, you have to see "Lost Romance," The guy is Marcus Chang—soooo guapo! The leading girl is not a looker but her personality will grow on you.

Oh, really, Mark Chang is really handsome.

I am almost done with "Record of Youth" with Park Bo Gum! He is handsome. I loved him in the "Moonlight Drawn by Clouds." He is very young, though. I just like good-looking leads.

I do not like Korean. The handsome males look effeminate with chiseled features.

Yes, like "Rookie Historian"—so guapo but too pretty.

Wait, let me write all these titles on a piece of paper.

MAHJONG!

Panigit, 60, rota there 789-789-789, plus 50, and double dice: $2.20!

If she mahjongs again, that is a clean table! Plus 50! $1!

The sound of "washing mahjong tiles" (shuffling the tiles) brings me back to Hongkong, my home for 13 years in the 1980s, where restaurants in the Kowloon side closed up after dinner to be transformed into mahjong parlors until four or five in the morning, and where the reverberation of "washing" sounds interrupted the street clamor of nighttime hawkers.

Personally, I am propelled back into my grandmother's time, circa 1950s where her sala and family room metamorphosed into a mahjong parlor of two to three tables on weekends. My cousins and I have grown up hearing Spanish conversations—politics, neighborhood gossip, and problems with the help, ad nauseam. We were not allowed to play the game, however, but we could be mirons. That was how I learned the game—as an onlooker, beside my aunt or my grandma. I remember my old Tito Vicente, known for throwing invectives when he made a wrong move: Puneta! was his signature expletive. As if it was not offensive enough, several times, his dentures would eject across the table with the blaring curse, everyone cringing from the explosion of both the profanity and spray of saliva.

One of the players was an old Chinese little person, who everyone called Pandac and whose bound feet mesmerized my cousins and me, that when a tile fell to the floor below where she sat, we plunged under the table in no time to pick up the tile so we could examine her miniscule feet up close!

The most memorable part of those miron times, for us youngsters, was the merienda prepared by my grandma.

Food is one of the best happenings of our mahjong sessions as well. Many a Filipina expatriate has become adept at culinary arts. I'd like to think that I inherited my grandma's Pampango proclivity for cooking delicious food. Even with helpers back in Hongkong, Taiwan, and Singapore, which were my previous places of residence, I personally managed the kitchen, especially when we entertained. Like my grandma, I

186

usually cook without recipes, concocting dishes I have tasted, and following the trail of my inherited gustatory instincts. Because of our weekly ritual of mahjong with food, Carla has become another kitchen goddess, following "Panlasang Pinoy" recipes found on the Internet and coming up with new gastronomic medley of dishes.

Callos this Wednesday from Carla's kitchen, plus French bread and balsamic and oil dip from Bing, salad and ahi spread from Margot, and my homemade tiramisu.

Pepi and Lita complete our alternating quorum. Viki, Tubi, Amazon, and Netflix manage to punctuate our seven-hour ecstasy on Tuesdays or Wednesdays, when Bing is not attending to her many business ventures.

After our gastronomic feast, our punctilious guanli yuan Bing, who wants to start "en punto!" leads us to our cozy, air-conditioned gallery where another feast transpires—an amalgam of well-crafted female shapes by Margot's late artist husband and former *Honolulu Advertiser* cartoonist Dick Adair, a splash of colors from floral throw pillows, and lush emerald plants.

After the first high, Laoshi Carla, our indefatigable mahjong expert, leads our placement:

Choose a tile. This is the east—you are there, Margot, Bing here, Nanette across Bing, and I sit here!

Mahjong was developed during the Qing dynasty in China and could have been brought to our shores by Limahong, a Chinese pirate and warlord who invaded the northern Philippine islands in 1574. Chinese merchants who sought their fortune in other parts of Asia and founded the large Chinese-Filipino communities may also have perpetuated the game, gambling tables becoming enterprising ventures in the 1900s.

For many Americans, mahjong evokes images of old mustachioed men and elderly women sitting around a square

187

table. I sometimes imagine Limahong's army of 3,000 outlaws, pirates, and bandits resorting to mahjong in their hideouts all over Luzon after their run-ins with the Spanish commanders, gambling away the nights with the gold they commandeered from the Spanish Armada. Or in some conspiracy and business circles, perhaps Spanish and Chinese warlords have secretly bonded to play this "cultural exchange."

Annelise Heinz from Stanford's History Department has found that Jewish-American and Chinese-American communities were built around mahjong in the 1920s. Imagine friends in a Chinatown apartment building in San Francisco or in a Jewish Brooklyn home in the 1950s, strengthening their bonds of social interaction. Her research reports that mahjong has created a shared heritage among Chinese Americans and among American Jewish women when many Americans saw them as "perpetual foreigners."

Unbeknownst to many, Filipino homes have been happily raucous with this pastime decades before. The Filipino mahjong borrowed its origins from the Chinese game, but instead of 13 tiles, it uses 16. While the Chinese use the flowers, winds, and dragons as suits, the Filipino mahjong regards all of these as "flowers," and acquisition of such chalked up the winner's yield. Each culture enhanced and developed its own rules, customs, and idiosyncratic practices.

The Filipino mahjong social network transcended cultural backgrounds. Hence, my grandma's quorum was a mix of Filipino, Spanish, Chinese descendants who have converged at the mahjong table through births, marriages, and deaths, perpetuating their bonds. Our quorum of former colegiala-expatriate women follows the mold.

Just as mahjong brought together my grandma and her friends and kept them intact through the years, so is it also a glue that keeps Bing, Carla, Lita, Margot, Pepi, and me in touch with our daily activities, and we gush in and out in quadruple languages.

Indeed, mahjong is an extension of the language learning app, "Babbel," and a reflection of the Filipinos' heritage. Three centuries of Spanish rule have influenced our vernacular, and our mahjong terminology like escalera, siete pares, sin ter, todo pong, mano, etc. are juxtaposed with Filipino terms, bunot, paningit, harang, besides the actual Chinese terms of pong, chow, kung.

Mahjongeras: Carla Lita, Pepi, and Nanette.

Because of our penchant for Chinese and Korean dramas of late, Chinese and Korean words have spiced up our conversations: Annyeonghaseyo, amigas! Laoshi, chifu, I like your blouse! Kitari. anyo. Ni shuo shenme? Wo bu dong are some of our spurted lexicon which accentuate our efforts to meld more drama into our game.

It was the afternoon mahjong sessions six decades ago which transformed my former nanny-turned-celebrated chef of my grandma as her amigas' extended Spanish student. Nanay Seriang was a no-read-no-write middle-aged woman turned mayordoma of my grandma, but her Spanish was impeccable due to the weekend mahjong sessions of my grandma's Spanish-speaking quorum!

"Como se dice puede na kayo mag merienda, Señora Montsi?" Nanay Seriang would eagerly ask. After months, years? of "como se dice," Nanay Seriang incrementally increased her Spanish vocabulary and perfectly enunciated a Castillian accent. "No toques las fichas de mahjong, ninos," she would admonish us not to touch the mahjong chips, in a grand old lady fashion.

My Lola Ediong is dancing in her grave knowing I have picked up on her favorite pastime in the distant shores of Honolulu, not as a miron, but as part of an earlier quorum with Lita, Pepi, and Carla some four years ago. Our routine emulates that of my grandma's time with a "call to begin" usually at 1:00 in the afternoon, a merienda break, and a last high before seven, and dinner, if we have leftovers.

Just like then, our time together is diced with lots of kwentuhan and chismis, usually of Filipino alta sociedad and politics, as are probably dramatized in other Filipino mahjong tables at present.

There is definitely a bond among our quorum. We have become kindred spirits, taking turns cooking and hosting, sharing and reminiscing about our own family traditions, childhood, travels, and experiences of our education in Manila convent schools. We think of each other with favorite dishes and chichirias, latest fashion trends (with Margot's often generous tendency to dole out her slightly used or never-worn pricey outfits whenever she visits her wardrobe to Bing's and my delight!), and text each other regularly about titles of novels and the Korean and Chinese dramas we enjoyed. We have added lunch, theater, and shopping trips outside mahjong days, feeling like colegialas again while recalling times we dated in college. Mahjong is indeed a re-creation!

As mahjong has transcended generational boundaries, I have also shared this past time with my haole husband Jim, who plays the Chinese version with our neighbors, and to my sons Juan Miguel and Ignacio, gifting them a set each for Christmas, hoping they would find the same joy in sitting together at a mahjong table. One night, during our California Christmas reunion, we played the game until one a.m., as Migz refused to stop without a single mahjong. He could not believe that his wife Teenah's fortune (she had won about 20 games at this point!) was induced by her lucky seat. After 34 games and much cajoling by the rest of us, he finally succumbed and moved to Teenah's spot AND finally made his first mahjong! We got to go to bed.

Here in Honolulu, we've had "magic" lucky seats. Margot has a different strategy. She "wakes up" Dick when her fitchas are dwindling. "Adair, wake up! I am losing!" As if Dick is resurrected, Margot makes mahjong!

MAHJONG!! All up.

Teka, nga, let me call Jim too! Honey, how are you? I am losing but enjoying our chit chat and Korean and Chinese history updates.

Okay to lose, Honey, as long as you are enjoying yourself!

MAHJONG! "

Wow, that strategy really works, Margot.

Wait, I have not come out for two highs! Let me go around my chair!

I think that would work. You are changing the energy, instructs Pepi.

And like a charm….

191

MAHJONG!

Wow, so fast—almost before the fifth—and double dice!

When will we eat the rest of the tiramisu?

Clearly, my Honolulu mahjong has transported me back and forth between my grandma's sala in Ermita and our homes in Honolulu, and the memories intertwine with the present...

Ay amigas! Esto es mi evento favorito—la merienda de Ediong!

Como se hace esta salsa de bechamel?

You should have Nanette's adobo. It is the bomb. What do you put in it, Nette?

Nothing special. It is just like everyone's adobo—vinegar, soy sauce, peppercorn, and bay leaves, but my grandma says, "Do not hesitate to put loads of garlic!" The secret also lies in the balance your palate contrives of the sour and salty blend—and then fry the meat pieces to brown them, then pour in the warm sauce as you serve the dish.

I wonder if my grandma is smiling as she watches over me, her first granddaughter (and my cousins say, her favorite), arranging mahjong tiles meticulously, although I cannot ever unseat our Laoshi Carla from her throne.

So, I now am a grandma myself, and my grandchildren will probably remember that I gifted them a mahjong set, offsetting an internal generational divide. My youngest son Nacho's family in Philadelphia has been playing it during the Covid interlude. Second son Migz' second daughter Mia, at six years old, knows all the suits—balls, bamboo, characters, but the flowers confuse her. Because of her heritage, (mom Teenah is an American-born Taiwanese), Mia can recognize the Chinese characters better than I can, sans the Arabic numerals. Both my sons had played mahjong at Taipei American School with

Chinese-American classmates, mahjong being the most popular group game during "class nights."

As a young girl watching and observing my grandma's friends, I thought mahjong was just a game for old people who had nothing better to do. Now that it has clearly transcended time, place, age, and culture, I realize that my time with my amigas goes beyond our favorite recipes, novels, playing pickleball, Chinese and K-drama reviews, memories of our mothers, titas and lolas, side lessons on history, languages, real life drama, real and reel "affairs," and growing mahjong strategies and vocabulary, etc. I have appreciated it as an enjoyable intellectual challenge, a way to rekindle our past and celebrate our cultural heritage, and a catalyst in strengthening the very important Filipino value of personal relationships in our final migrant home.

Mahjong has spiced our expatriate lives with food, drama, and life…and has honored the shared heritage we have kept alive.

Translations can be found in the Glossary.

*Upon graduating from St. Theresa's College, Manila, **Nanette Carreon-Ruhter** taught at San Beda College and the Ateneo University in Manila. After completing her master's degrees from Ateneo University and UC Berkeley, Nanette taught English Literature and Writing at Hong Kong International School, Taipei American School, and Singapore American School, and directed writing workshops for UC Berkeley and the East Asia Writing Project for international school teachers in the1980s and 1990s. Now retired, she does substitute teaching at Punahou and Iolani schools, and Le Jardin Academy. She and her husband Jim live in Honolulu.*

Twenty Two

JO KOY AND ME

by Pepi Nieva

"Who or what is a JoKoy?" asked my octogenarian friend.

You might surmise one must be over 80 and/or non-Filipino to NOT know of Jo Koy, arguably the most recognized Fil-Am comedian of all time. I was like them, too until 2017 when, alongside his Netflix special debut, the Filipino-American comic with a heavy leaning towards his mom's Pinoy side, sold out 11 shows in Honolulu's largest venue with a record 23,000 people (excluding me) buying tickets. Since then, Jo Koy's brand of stand-up comedy has been playing to full houses from San Francisco to Dubai. In 2019, he placed first on the Billboard Charts for his stand-up comedy album, "Live From Seattle."

When my Facebook feed began pointing me towards Jo Koy's videos on YouTube, I found that from one to eight million viewers were tuning into his shticks about the time he had to go to school with a Cool Whip tub masquerading as Tupperware for his munggo and patis home lunch; his mom's cure-all, Vicks Vaporub; how Pinoys point with their lips and confuse their *p*s and *f*s and *v*s and *b*s (Louis Buitton!).

Why are people amused at things that are true? I thought. Maybe Filipinos, who make up a substantial and loyal portion of Jo Koy's fan base, recognize the jokes as kantiyawan, an almost

194

Jo Koy and (photoshopped) me at "Easter Sunday" premiere.

always good-natured teasing behavior common among friends in the old country. Perhaps coming together to laugh is a way of strengthening Pinoys' already strong social bonds, a phenomenon mentioned in scholarly humor studies.

Or are audiences laughing simply because Jo Koy, with his excellent timing and delivery and hyperkinetic body language, is a skilled storyteller of ethnic stereotypes that have been part and parcel of many comedians' humor arsenal for decades?

Afterall, Jo Koy's audience can't be all Filipino—his social media followers count much more than the four million Filipino population in America and the approximately two million OFWs across the world (but of course not Filipinos in the Philippines).

Stereotypes are defined by sociologists as generalized "beliefs about typical characteristics of members of certain ethnic groups, their status, societal, and cultural norms," according to the Dictionary of Psychology. Stereotypes can be derogatory and lead to discrimination; in the earlier days of Filipino immigration to America, Filipinos were thought to eat dog and, in Hawai'i, to "poke knife" (get into fights), for instance. On the other hand, stereotypes can be useful in increasing understanding of other people and ourselves.

But are stereotypes accurate and true? And if generally so, what are the values and circumstances that push a group of people towards their purported stereotypical behavior?

To find out, I turned to the most convenient focus group I could find: my friends and me.

Mom

My mom had to raise us on her own. Tough as ****. The only language she talked was yell! Hah? When did you do it? Where? Where did you go? Hah?!? What?!?!!

Everyone who's watched Jo Koy knows that his mom is his act's central figure. Koy's is a strong, feisty, no-nonsense single mother who instilled fear and discipline in her son's life. Jo Koy and his mom both say his stories are true-to-life, although she doesn't curse as much as her stage persona.

So what happened to the image (stereotype) of the subservient and demure Filipina/Asian woman?

When I was in college, my thesis revolved around the pre-Hispanic Filipina, based on reports by Spanish chroniclers who first set foot on the islands that would become the Philippines. Equal in most respects with men, she could work and move around freely; own property and conduct financial transactions; marry and divorce when she pleased, serve as a spiritual guide and healer; and inherit her father's leadership role in her community. The obedient, devout, and meek Filipina model, formed by 300 years of indoctrination into the Spanish colonial female ideal, still exists, but not in Jo Koy's or my family. My mom was a civic leader who instilled fear in the people who helped in her advocacies, even if they were just volunteers. She would have done the same for us if we weren't three girls in a row who had each other for protection.

One could argue that the Philippines is a matriarchal society underneath its veneer of macho patriarchy; women traditionally control household finances and wield influence, even if behind the scenes, in political, economic, and social matters. As far as equal opportunity, according to the Global Gender Gap Report of 2014, the Philippines is ranked ninth in the world and was the only Asian country in the global top 50, writes Dr. Michael Daniels, assistant professor at the University of British Columbia, in his article "The Gender Gap: What Asia Can Learn from the Philippines." He goes on to report that the Philippines leads Southeast Asian countries in terms of women's educational attainment and presence in senior management. Globally, the country ranks fifth in the world with women occupying 37 percent of management roles; the global average is 19 percent. And the Philippines already has two female presidents versus zero in the U.S.

Says Edna, a nurse and professor, "Women are the toughest creatures on earth. Pinoy women bring a lot of structure to their family. They are resilient and find ways to always bring out the best in people even though they are very strict, especially with their children."

I'll take that kind of stereotype.

Go back! Get Extra!

> *Go back in there and get extra napkins…She hands out napkins. None of them match. KFC, McDonald's, Taco Bell, Burger King, Cheesecake Factory. Oh, that's a good one—It's a lot thicker than the others.*

Hey, I do that, too! Even if I didn't use them at my kids' birthday parties or any parties, just for everyday use so I don't run out of the store-bought kind. Grace "gets extra" plastic bags. She asks the waitress for more at Cheesecake Factory where the bags are better than the supermarket type. Her mom Rose folds her bags into neat triangles. I collect plastic bags, too, to reuse as bathroom trash liners. I bring them disguised as baggage stuffing to Hawai'i, when it started charging for grocery bags before Oregon, my second home, did. The sturdier, nicely designed plastic and paper bags are in two big bins in my dressing room for who knows what emergency use.

Then there's my equivalent of Jo Koy's Cool Whip lunch box. I have plastic containers of varying kinds in the cupboard for after-party take-home packaging and leftovers. With recycling, I don't feel bad throwing some away.

198

Why do many Filipinos place such great value on Reducing Reusing and Recycling?

We were trained from childhood. When we were growing up in Manila, we had newspaper drives in schools or the paper collector man would come to the house to gather old periodicals neatly tied together with rope. The school and the collector man could then exchange the papers for cash. Every time we bought soft drinks in glass bottles, we would be sure to return them to get our deposit; I hear that nowadays the neighborhood store pours the drinks into plastic bags with straws and just keeps the bottles. At our big teenage parties, complete with "combos" or four-person live bands, the paper plates were lined with even more disposable wax paper and reused at the next event.

We are also experts in making do with what's available. My husband and American-raised sons won't do a task without the right tools. I find paraan—a way to improvise with whatever is on hand. While the results may not be ideal, it gets the job done until a more permanent fix can be found.

People in developing countries don't have the luxury of throwing away something that might not be available, is expensive, or still suitable for a second, third, or fourth repurposed life. Waste not, want not. It's a value that's evolved from our shared circumstances and environment. We "get extra" just in case.

Balikbayan Box

As broke as my mom was, twice a year, she would fill up a balikbayan box and send it to her family back home. She would fill it with stuff (like chocolate) I wish I could have had!

--Jo Koy on including the balikbayan box in "Easter Sunday," New York Times *interview, August 9, 2022.*

JO KOY MIXED PLATE
A BOOK REVIEW

By Rose Cruz Churma
Originally published in the *Hawaii Filipino Chronicle*

On the flap of the book's cover, Jo Koy notes, "Here is the path to my American Dream...And I want to make you laugh while I do it. I'm like Hawai'i's favorite lunch—the mixed plate. Little bit of this, a little bit of that. Mixed Plate is too."

Jo Koy, born Joseph Glen Herbert to a Filipina immigrant mom and white American dad, is one of Hawai'i's favorite stand-up comics, and perhaps, the rest of the world where Filipinos live—or where folks believe in reaching out for their dreams.

His stand-up comic monologues gained traction with Filipinos when he poked fun at his immigrant experience—especially when he describes incidents with his Filipina mom. It resonated with folks who were brought up with a mother I'd call an immigrant "Everymom" trying to acculturate in their new adopted home, and in pursuit of the American dream for themselves and their children.

He has a keen sense of observation and in the retelling of his family's journey, this book is also a social commentary on what it is to be a Filipino-American during the past 50 years or so, particularly for one who is of mixed parentage.

But his book also chronicles his personal story of a bi-racial kid growing up around military bases in white America, a college drop-out who could not fulfill his mother's dreams of acquiring a salaried, stable, and dependable job—as a nurse, for example. Although the context of his acts revolve around his Filipino-American upbringing, the story he shares is universal.

This is why, in his shows, the audience is diverse: his stories are relatable, no matter your ethnicity.

His concerts here in Hawai'i were mostly sold-out, so that 2021's events were moved from the Blaisdell's concert hall to the arena—a larger venue. And even then, they had to add another show. It was this added show, on a Sunday evening, that I was finally able to watch Jo Koy in the flesh! I was the third wheel to my daughter's night out with her beau. Parts of the concert were very uncomfortable for me—those jokes that I thought verged on the vulgar, or the constant use of the "F' word (after all I am a baby-boomer brought up devoutly Catholic). Although the book is liberally laced with the same words and sounds like him on stage, in the printed form, it is a better format for me. It's like having Jo Koy in your living room sharing his life story—better than watching his Netflix special!

Interestingly, the book also contains several recipes of—I assume—Jo Koy's favorite Filipino dishes: lumpia, shrimp sinigang, pancit, chicken wings adobo, and halo-halo. I will try his chicken wings adobo and its boiled egg garnish; the wings are fried first and then baked with the adobo sauce and eaten with freshly steamed rice. Prepare this dish one rainy day, get a copy of this book and enjoy!

Ah, the balikbayan box! That 24" x 18" x 24" cardboard carrier that's launched many a door-to-door freight delivery business catering to Filipinos in diaspora who habitually send care packages back home.

Why not send money instead? Companies like LBC and Atlas do that too at a much cheaper rate than UPS and Fedex. Carla's Japanese friend, while watching "Easter Sunday," the first Hollywood-produced movie starring Jo Koy and an all-Filipino cast (except two), found some similarities about sending gifts back to the old country; she sends money orders, not a box full of stuff.

Filipinos, though, appear to shop with their recipients lovingly in mind. My housekeeper Linda, who's always at the remittance counter sending her hard-earned dollars to relatives who are sick, need money for funerals, tuition, new business ventures, etc. etc., regularly packs balikbayan boxes (cost: $60 from Hawai'i to the Philippines) full of food, clothing, diapers, and more. She says money might go to other uses, versus hard goods that relatives definitely need. I once met some Filipinas buying cases of Vienna sausage on sale at Longs, Hawai'i's favorite drug and sundry store, for their balikbayan box.

My friends Margot and Nanette collect clothes, shoes, and other useful things for less fortunate relatives in the provinces, a common practice especially when typhoons and other natural disasters hit the country. At the airport, you can spot the Filipinos because their luggage consists of balikbayan boxes which, sized to fit airline baggage requirements, can contain much more pasalubong (gifts from travels, identical to the Japanese omiyage) than the ordinary suitcase.

You'd be surprised at the things you can find in a balikbayan box. A friend (name withheld as a safeguard) spirited her mother's and father's ashes inside a balikbayan box. It was easier than going through the paperwork required by the Philippine government to repatriate remains of the deceased!

Clearly, the balikbayan box is as a tangible manifestation of the value of family, and the desire to help others (kapwa).

All Your Cousins are Nurses

Filipino moms predetermine what their kids are supposed to be when they grow up. You know I'm not making this *** up. There are a lot of Filipinos here right now that are nurses. This is a good time to be injured at a show!

Why are there so many Filipina nurses in hospitals around the world? The answer, like that of the balikbayan box, is family. To put an offspring (usually a daughter) through nursing school is seen by Filipinos as an almost sure-fire ticket to a well-paid, stable job "abroad." Philippine nursing websites list the U.S., Saudi Arabia, Canada, the United Kingdom, Germany, and Singapore as desirable destinations for immigrating nurses. From these overseas stations, the dutiful daughter can support her family and even bring some of them over to the promised, higher-wage lands.

Tita Elising was one of the pioneer nurse recruiters in the Philippines. After working as a surgical and public health nurse, she founded a travel agency to help with medical shortages in the East Coast and the Midwest in the 1960s. Her "Exchange Visitors/Fly Now Pay Later" program offered two-year contracts to nurses and doctors in large hospitals in the U.S. Her eldest daughter, Beth, became a nurse too. Violeta, now a successful health care businesswoman in Honolulu, came to America as a nurse recruit for a major New York institution, where she bravely fought for equal rights for foreign health workers. Despite sometimes stringent licensing requirements, nurses continue to contribute to the diaspora. Surveys show that the Philippines is the largest foreign exporter of nurses to the United States, where their dedication to caring for others has been recognized especially during the pandemic.

"There is value in why Pinoys encourage their children to be nurses," says nurse/professor Edna. "But I always thought I would have been a professional dancer."

Do the Michael Jackson

When she found out I could dance like Michael Jackson, she made me do it every time someone came to the house. Josep, your uncle is here. Do the Michael Jackson (stamps feet).

When we were young, my mother made us perform for the relatives. I hated that! So much so I don't remember what we sang; I don't think we danced. We were also forced to take piano lessons with mother as our teacher. Piano was her college major.

As a result, I never demanded that my children do the Michael Jackson or anything else. Nowadays, though, oldest son sings karaoke and younger son plays the guitar. And I sing and play the ukulele and dance a bit of hula. We'll attribute that to the Filipino's inherent propensity for music and dance, already noted centuries ago in Spanish chronicles.

Tabo, Rice, and Other Truisms

Jo Koy has a YouTube "PSA" about avoiding the Covid-induced toilet paper shortage with the tabo—the little plastic tub with a handle used as a basic bidet in lots of Filipino households, even second-generation ones. What did Hawai'i-born-and-raised Apol buy on our trip to the Baguio market? Two tabos to bring back home.

To take the place of tabo, I've installed sprayers and bidets in my house ("What's that?" asked a haole friend who obviously hasn't sat over oscillating water from heated Toto toilet seats found in hotels catering to Japanese and other Asians). But when traveling, I've been known to use a drinking glass as a tabo, or better yet, a water bottle.

I also deploy the finger tool. You don't need measuring cups when cooking rice. Just add water to the first line of your third finger (or really, any finger). You can buy Jo Koy-brand tabo and rice on his website.

Someone gave me a tiny Sto. Nino (Infant Jesus of Prague), smaller than the one in the "Easter Sunday" movie. It's perched on a chest in my dining room, although it can never replace the family's heirloom statue with the ivory head and hands that we sold to an antique dealer in Manila.

One thing I don't have is pride in my favorite recipes. I don't have any, but I truly enjoy those prepared by friends who do cook.

Can We See Ourselves Better Now?

"Easter Sunday," produced with the support of Steven Spielberg and distributed by Universal, is the first mainstream film about Filipinos—a milestone for Filipino and Asian-American communities in America. With a $17 million budget, it brought in $5.4 million during its opening weekend, within the projections for non-blockbuster type movies. Reviews have come in mixed. Some critics and viewers felt that while the movie is a good exercise in representing Filipino culture, the jokes and situations could have been better presented.

Jo Koy calls "Easter Sunday" his love song to his people. He says he's on a mission to make sure Filipinos are represented in the media. "That's why I hold this flag up so high and this is why it's so important for something like this ("Easter Sunday") to come out because there are kids like me, or there are kids still to this day just trying to find their identity or hear their voice. They feel invisible and this movie's gonna give them a sense of identity," he says in an interview on *Cinema Blend*.

As for those who say his humor is too specific to being Filipino to succeed, Jo Koy counters with the title of his new world tour: "Funny is Funny." He asserts that his audience demographic is a mix of ethnicities. There are no ethnic profiles available for Jo Koy Netflix specials or live shows, but the opening night audience for "Easter Sunday" was 37 percent Asian, 31 percent Caucasian, 15 percent Latino, and 11 percent African-American, with women coming in at 55 percent of the total, according to *Deadline*, a Hollywood news site.

"Hilarioius! I laughed aloud," is the verdict of a tough critic, Kathleen, a non-Filipino theater director who had never heard or seen Jo Koy until my so-called focus group.

"I love Jo Koy. I think his jokes are relatable even if you're not Filipino," says Theresia. "My non-Filipino husband loves all his jokes, too. He says his mother also did the Cool Whip as Tupperware, but not to the extent of Jo Koy's mom. I think he's just telling me stories about his family life. I don't really feel he's telling me ALL Filipinos are alike."

"My husband, who is African-American, actually introduced me to Jo Koy on Netflix," relates Edna. "He always points at me when Jo Koy says something that resonates with him about me and my family."

"I think there's truth to his jokes, that's why people can relate to them," agrees Kit.

When Alma and her family emerged from an "Easter Sunday" viewing, they embarked on serious discussions on the authenticity of the movie's characterization of Filipinos and their culture. Because it is a breakthrough first, people expect it to represent culture accurately, respectfully, and unrealistically, perfectly. Authenticity is crucial because how we are represented in influential media affects how others perceive us, as well as how we perceive and value ourselves.

Grace, a millennial from Hawai'i now living in Texas, has seen three of Jo Koy's live shows, the movie, and dozens of videos. She feels Jo Koy's work recognizes and brings light to Filipinos and increases our sense of community and pride.

Karen, a second-generation Filipina living in New York, thought "Easter Sunday" was funny in some parts and although it was not well-written, she would still recommend it for the vignettes of Filipino culture.

Kainoa, a teenager who's half Filipino and half Laotian, says that even if some jokes are stereotypical, there should be more movies like "Easter Sunday."

Jo Koy's comedy may not be everyone's ideal cup of salabat. I, personally, don't like the vulgar parts of his routine. Online haters accuse Jo Koy of cultural appropriation to make a buck, noting he's only half Filipino. Some Filipinos think the comic is making fun of their accents. Jo Koy's portrayal of our kababayan can't be an accurate representation of every Filipino. But it has raised awareness of being Filipino in America. That's valuable to me. Ask your own focus groups if it is for them, too.

Pepi Nieva is a writer and public relations professional who lives in Honolulu and Oregon. She grew up in Manila and immigrated to Hawai'i in the mid 1970s. She spends her retirement years traveling, visiting with friends and family, and playing the ukulele.

Twenty Three

THIS IS NOT MY DREAM

by Ashley Valois

That is not my dream, I say.
"Get money. Fast education. Become a nurse."
Kunana jay nanang ko. (My mother says)
"Haan ko kayat mut," I plead. (I do not want
to)

The strong, unwavering gaze looms over me.
A delicate dark cloth traps my mouth.
I bow my head in misery.
Enveloped in thoughts of white walls,
the chatter of healing jargon,
the smell of blood, urine, and dying souls fill my sensitive
nostrils.

I raise my head
that will not be
me. I raise my
head
Ripping away the hand that holds my throat
and say "No."
My dream will be my own.

Ashley Valois wrote this poem based on numerous conversations with her parents. Before she was born in the Philippines, her father supported the family by working on a cruise ship and her mother as a nanny in Hong Kong. At five years old, she and her mother immigrated to Hawai'i.

As a Filipina and the eldest child, she knows she has a responsibility to take care of her parents and provide for them, in addition to taking care of her siblings. Yet, there have been consistent arguments that concern careers and life ambitions. Her parents urged her to become a nurse since it was a stable and good-paying job. She struggled between choosing the duty to her family and the duty to herself.

She is currently majoring in political science and intends to go to law school.

Twenty Four

BROWN

by Gloriani Lontoc

I was born on an island. An island familiar to the sweep of its sun. In the Philippines, the sun penetrated the atmosphere and cradled you like a Christmas lechon. It was a heat that bleached the billboards and simultaneously stained your shirt with pawis. The sun was persistent and desperate to feel our skin, to soak in our melanin. But we reject the sun, the burning force that shone for billions of years, the light that travelled thousands of miles just to get a glimpse of the same shade of sepia that our ancestors also had.

We resist the sun for its detriment to the fair skin that colonizers convinced us was the model of divinity. We rejected its attempts to remain resilient against the tree tops and tin roofs to land on our face all the way from planets away because we are afraid of the brown that nature created. We feared a sun that represents liberty, the very sun that shines on our national flag and the rays that revolted against the very colonizers that led us to believe that God did not favor the color he chose to build the mountains and land that held the seas.

Well, I was raised on an island, an island that fed the sun to me with a different spoon and the same hand. Unlike most places I have learned to know, the Polynesian sun favored its people. For the first time in my life, I found a community that embraced, chased, and lived by the position of its star. Hawai'i had the sun that I grew up in, the one that was transported by the trade winds and laced with the sweetness of the sea. My skin was bronzed by the breeze that carried its light through our open windows.

But our Filipino households remained shut. *No light should touch the skin that goes outside.* It did not matter how much fun I had outside that day nor how far I swam at the beach. It did not matter what goal I scored at soccer nor the good news I ran home for instead of catching the bus. *It simply did not matter.* My titos still squinted in my direction, joking that I was so dark that they could not see me. My titas pitied this dirt-stained little girl and recommended papaya soaps to my mom. My lola would hold me and tell me that I smelled like the sun.

Because of this, I would soak the lining of my long sleeve shirts in the sweat of hormones and heat. My jeans were faded from all the daily washes I begged my mom for. I wore the same, sad cardigan over and over just to shield my skin. My accomplishments, my beauty and successes as a person sat dormant in the shade of the pressure to be light, *to be pretty.*

My mom told me that brown was beautiful. She said that this was the brown that birthed me, the same shade that got a degree and travelled around the world. It was the shade of brown that hugs me on my good days and bad days and it was a brown that she was proud of and loves. But I felt like it was an obligation to love me, that *my* brown was deep and disgusting. I was so desperate for the approval of a community that told me to be proud of my country while simultaneously shaming me because I embodied a hallmark of its people...and so I put the papaya soap to my face.

I declined invitations to the beach, refrained from going to the pool despite the summer attempts to cool me, I simply pretended like I had better things to do. I did not want to be dark, I did not want to smell like the sun, and so I compromised and I ended up sacrificing my childhood wading in the shade because being fair-skinned was far better than having fun.

But now I live on island, an island in the Atlantic, but an island no less. I sit here 25 years since leaving my original islands of the Philippines and 11 years since Hawai'i, cold and desperate for a glimpse of the sun. In England, we get a week or two of good sunlight. That is to say that some clouds are present and the rays of the sun are not directly piercing your soul. There is no breeze, there is no moisture, it is just you, the sun, and the hopes that you will survive without leathering (I got my first sunburn out here). I moved here in my twenties anticipating a culture shock where I would wallow in the novelty of being surrounded by something different for once. I wanted to be a part of the crowd, I wanted to fit in so badly. However, just like my lack of sunscreen, I was unprepared for living on this island and continent.

It took me nearly a quarter of a decade to realize that we are not a people meant to fit in. That being kissed by a sun is not a detriment to our successes. That we are challenged with enough adversities of being a minority that we need not do it to our own kind.

I learned that brown skin in itself was a novelty to the rest of the world. Where we in the Philippines are so adamant about being fair-skinned, our counterparts in Europe are paying for vacations and subscriptions just to be smirked at by the sun. Whereas we once pitied the sweat that rolled down the backs of slaves and farmers, we somehow associated the hard work and grit of the Filipino people with the scorn of the sun. We developed a distaste in the proof of our labors, a visual representation of our victory as the Filipino people, the color of our roots and many roots alike.

Our culture is bountiful with reasons to be proud and being brown should be one of them. We are a hardworking and ambitious people with a tenacity that is unmatched. We are blessed with our brown skin, we are blessed as Filipino. It does not matter what we do or where we are, *it simply does not matter*. We are Filipino and the sun shines down on us.

Gloriani "Keeyan" Lontoc was born in Cavite City and grew up in Honolulu. She is a U.S. Air Force non-commissioned officer in charge of Anatomical Pathology at the Royal Air Force Lakenheath, UK.

Since joining the US Air Force, she has garnered various awards including the Levitow Award for the top graduate, and the US Air Force Europe and Africa non-commissioned officer of the year award. She was named her squadron's volunteer of the year for raising funds in support of organizations dedicated to preserving the environment and human rights. She also coordinated the collection and distribution of thousands of masks for those affected by the Taal Volcano eruption and for medical personnel involved in the Covid pandemic in the Philippines.

GLOSSARY

1.	Adobo (Pilipino)	vinegar and soy-sauce flavored dish
2.	Alta sociedad (Spanish)	high society
3.	Amin (Cebuano)	kiss hand as sign of respect
4.	Amo (Pilipino)	master
5.	Annyeonghaseyo (Korean)	hello
6.	Anyo (Korean)	no
7.	Anito (Pilipino)	spirit guardian
8.	Ate (Pilipino)	older sister
9.	Atsay/Tsimay (Pilipino)	maid
10.	Babaylan (Pilipino)	priestess, healer
11.	Bunot (Pilipino)	draw
12.	Chichirias (Pilipino)	snacks
13.	Chismis (Pilipino	gossip
14.	Chow (Chinese)	three of a kind
15.	Colegiala (Spanish)	college girl
16.	Como se dice (Spanish)	how do you say
17.	Como se hace (Spanish)	how do you make
18.	En punto (Spanish)	right on the dot
19.	Fichas (Spanish)	money chips
20.	Gaba (Cebuano)	heaven's wrath
21.	Guanli yuan (Chinese)	administrator
22.	Guapo (Spanish)	good looking
23.	Halo halo (Pilipino)	mixed, icy dessert with many ingredients
24.	Haole (Hawaiian)	foreigner
25.	Ina (Pilipino)	mother
26.	Kababayan (Pilipino)	countryman
27.	Kitari (Korean)	wait
28.	Kung/kang (Chinese)	four of the same suit

29.	Kwentuhan (Pilipino)	chitchat, story telling
30.	Lola/Lolo (Pilipino)	grandmother/grandfather
31.	Laoshi, chifu (Chinese)	teacher, master
32.	Lechon (Spanish)	roast pig
33.	Lumpia (Pilipino)	eggroll
34.	Mabuhay (Pilipino)	long live
35.	Madrasta (Spanish, Pilipino)	stepmother
36.	Mano (Pilipino)	first, leader/hand
37.	Mayordoma (Spanish)	senior female butler
38.	Merienda (Spanish, Pilipino)	afternoon snack
39.	Miron (Spanish)	onlooker
40.	Muli (Pilipino)	again
41.	Ni shou shemme (Chinese)	what did you say?
42.	Ninang/Ninong (Pilipino)	godmother/godfather
43.	Palabok (Pilipino)	a thick noodle
44.	Pancit (Pilipino)	noodles
45.	Paningit (Pilipino)	in between tile
46.	Pasali naman (Pilipino)	let me join
47.	Patis (Pilipino)	fish sauce
48.	Pawis (Pilipino)	sweat
49.	Pogi (slang Pilipino)	handsome/guapo
50.	Pong (Chinese)	three of a kind
51.	Pwera usog (Pilipino)	go away, curse
52.	Querida (Spanish)	mistress
53.	Sala (Spanish, Pilipino)	living room
54.	Salabat (Pilipino)	ginger tea
55.	Salsa de bechamel (Spanish)	bechamel sauce
56.	Senorito (Spanish, Pilipino)	young master
57.	Siete pares (Spanish)	seven pairs
58.	Simhut (Cebuano)	inhaling kiss
59.	Sin ter (Spanish)	no terminal numeral
60.	Sinigang (Pilipino)	tamarind soup
61.	Teka nga (Pilipino)	wait a minute

62. Tita(s)/Tito(s) (Pilipino)   aunt(s)/uncle(s)
63. Todo pong (Spanish-Chinese) all three of a kind
64. Wo bu dong (Chinese)   I do not understand

Note:

This glossary contains terms that were not fully explained within the stories themselves. Pilipino is the Philippine national language and is sometimes referred to as Tagalog. Cebuano is the language of Cebu province.

ABOUT THE COVER

Eduardo Joaquin, Artist

Eduardo Joaquin is a contemporary figurative painter currently pursuing his Bachelors in Fine Arts with a focus on painting at the University of Hawai'i at Manoa. Joaquin has been the recipient of the John Young Scholarship, the Jean Charlot Foundation Scholarship, and the College of Arts and Letters Scholarship, He created a series of paintings for the Geraldine P. Clark Memorial Fellowship. His work has been exhibited at various venues in Hawai'i and published in the Leahi Creative Arts Journal.

The art for this book's cover, entitled "Rosa Maria," was included in the 2022 Schaefer Portrait Challenge, a statewide juried exhibition that has been held biennially on Maui since 2003. The prestigious exhibition aims to feature artists who best present the people of the islands.

"This opportunity allowed me to honor my mother and take time to be present with her as the matriarch who has always put family above herself," he says.

The description at the UH Manoa Commons Gallery, where he exhibited in December 2022, stated: Born in the Philippines but raised on Oahu from an early age, diasporic identity is central to Joaquin's work, bringing tension between his Filipino heritage and the Western academic tradition of oil painting. The gestural, disrupted forms of Joaquin's paintings are informed by narratives drawn from Philippine literature, the global art history canon, and current socio-political dialogues. Joaquin says, "Growing up as an immigrant, I've always had this desire to feel accepted in the space I occupy to the point of shedding any semblance of my background in hopes of assimilation. What I've come to realize is that I now no longer exist here nor there, stuck in a sort of cultural purgatory. I think that is something that I am trying to confront in my work."

He is working with FAUW on activities that support and promote art as an expression of culture.

ABOUT
THE FILIPINO ASSOCIATION OF UNIVERSITY WOMEN

FAUW

The Filipino Association of University Women (FAUW) was established in 1987 to promote and strengthen Filipino identity in Hawai'i through initiatives in culture, the arts, and education. Since its inception, the organization has provided leadership in promoting greater awareness of and appreciation for Filipino culture and values, and cross-cultural understanding in Hawai'i.

FAUW's programs include *Pasko!* a Christmas celebration; support for *Letters to My Parents,* which encourages students to communicate with their parents by writing; and the sponsorship of film festivals, art tours and exhibits, literacy projects, and cultural displays.

FAUW has partnered with organizations such as the Honolulu Museum of Arts, the Children's Discovery Center, the Filipino Community Center, the University of Hawai'i Center for Philippine Studies, the Philippine Consulate General of Hawai'i; the Friends of the Iolani Palace, and Reiyukai Hawai'i.

Its primary publications are *Student Speak,* an anthology of student writings (2022); *Pinay: Culture Bearers of the Filipino Diaspora* (2017); *Filipina* (1992); *Kayumanggi Presence* (1992); *Lola Basyang, Volumes 1 and 2,* DVD – various storytellers (2010 and 2011).

FAUW is a tax-exempt organization. Tax-deductible donations support FAUW projects and can be sent via PayPal (email: fauw1987@gmail.com).

For membership and more information, visit us on Facebook (FAUW) and our website: fauwhawaii.wordpress.com

218

Made in the USA
Las Vegas, NV
07 March 2023

68704352R00125